*To Rod*

# AWARD WINNING WINES

## Professional methods for the amateur winemaker

## Bill Smith

*I'm sorry there's only a cursory mention of malo-lactic in here, but I find that most amateur winemakers are not interested.*

*Bill*

**Nexus Special Interests**

Nexus Special Interests Ltd.
Nexus House
Azalea Drive
Swanley
Kent BR8 8HU
England

ISBN 1-85486-209-X

# CONTENTS

ACKNOWLEDGEMENTS

## ACKNOWLEDGEMENTS

My wife, Nancy, has given me support and encouragement throughout the writing of this book. In addition, I thank her for her excellent proof-reading and constructive advice.

I also thank the members, past and present, of Chilterns Masters Wine Guild for sharing my interest in developing recipes, and for sharing the load in making and tasting the experimental wines.

I thank all those who contributed recipes for this book, or allowed me to use data that has already been printed.

Finally, I am indebted to all the enthusiastic winemakers that I have met over the years, as the exchange and cross-fertilisation of ideas keeps winemaking interests at a high level.

# one
# INTRODUCTION

My first real introduction to wine was in California where I worked for five years in the 1960s. One of the social trips we used to make was to Napa Valley to visit the wineries. In those days, there were only eight wineries to visit. At my last count a few years ago, there were over 250! Over the years my involvement in wine has grown similarly. The days in California introduced me to the various styles of commercial wine available. However, on returning to England in 1968, beer was still the preferred beverage. It was a few years later that some wine kit presents at Christmas set me off on the winemaking trail. I was fortunate in having spent ten years working in the field of anaerobic fermentation. With this background in most of the skills necessary, winemaking was a natural extension.

Soon after, I joined a local wine club where I met other enthusiasts, and became engrossed in this new, fascinating hobby. I started entering competitions in shows, humbly learning that there was more to making good wine than simply conducting the fermentation properly. I was invited to join an elite group of winemakers who were interested in more than the average club could offer in the way of new challenges. My involvement in this group, and the methods we used to design recipes for different wine styles, are described in the chapter 'Recipe Design'. As my interest in home winemaking increased, so also did my interest in commercial wine. My wife and I started attending monthly wine tastings organised by the late Ted Adcock. We learned so much from these informative, inexpensive evenings. Slowly, our knowledge of the commercial scene increased, and really took off when we began cellaring good quality wines.

Having stewarded for wine judges at local shows, I became interested in the ability to grade wines in terms of quality. I became a member of The National Guild of Wine and Beer Judges, and was soon doing my share of the judging. I was invited to judge at the annual show of The National Guild of Wine and Beermakers, a show that we now look forward to visiting each year. From my first visit to my local Wine Circle to my annual trip to the National Show, I have made many friends in the winemaking world. Few hobbies offer such a genial bunch of comrades.

My reasons for this book are to harness the knowledge I have accrued over the years, and to record some of my ideas that have been put into practice in my own winemaking. Although this book contains sufficient information to allow the novice to start making wine, the main theme of the book is to show how improvements to standard techniques can be made, and to encourage the winemaker to experiment with new ideas. Readers with some experience in making wine will be familiar with such books as *Making Wines Like Those You Buy* and *Progressive Winemaking* by Bryan Acton and Peter Duncan. More recently, Professor Gerry Fowles has published Winemaking In Style and Must. The works of Acton and Duncan showed the amateur how to take the guesswork out of winemaking by using science and logic to blend fruits so that the final wine had a balance and flavour similar to the commercial. Gerry Fowles has continued to bridge the gap between the home winemaker and the professional vintner. Gerry's book Must is full of every conceivable fact about every fruit that could possibly be used to make wine. The purpose of this book is to complement these other works by demonstrating how the winemaker can, with time and patience, add significant improvements to the way that amateur wine is made.

The use of metabisulphite will be explained, allowing the winemaker to reduce the amounts used, and to end up with cleaner wines. Discussion of the blending of fruits and their timely addition will show how wines can be improved without changing the design of the basic recipe. One chapter shows how a small group of people can work together to develop a recipe that will produce a commercial style of wine. The use of various forms of oak, surely the biggest advance made in home winemaking in recent years, will be explained. Another chapter will demonstrate how one wine can be blended to make a selection of different wine styles, a short cut to entering many classes in a wine show. The methodology of making sparkling wines will be explained, from making the basic still wine to conducting the secondary fermentation, and following on to the remuage, disgorging, dosage addition, and maturation. Two chapters cover wine clubs, wine talks, and wine shows, the backbone of our national structure. The book concludes with a selection of 50 recipes from different sources. Some of these recipes are my own design, but I have incorporated other recipes from winemaking friends so that there is diversity in recipe design and winemaking style.

All the recipes are given in both imperial and metric units, the British pint being equal to 0.568 litres. The wine writers Acton and Duncan, and Gerry Fowles, have taken home winemaking well beyond the end of the 20th century. I hope that this book will help home winemaking to continue to flourish in the 21st century. All the recipes

# two
# THE BASIC EQUIPMENT

The following is a list of the essential equipment required to make wine successfully at home. The equipment can be bought at any shop that specialises in home wine and beer making, although such specialist shops may be hard to find in some areas. However, some large chain stores, such as Boots the Chemists, carry a sufficient range of winemaking equipment to satisfy the winemaker's needs.

## Glass fermenting jars

These are usually of approximately one-gallon capacity, and generally called demijohns. Here is one of the first of many minor problems that the winemaker can unwittingly encounter. I said 'approximately' one gallon, because most demijohns hold volumes nearer to 5 litres. A gallon is equal to 4.54 litres, but the mean volume held by eight of my gallon jars, when fitted with an airlock to give minimal air space, is 4.9 litres, an increase of 8%. Therefore, if a wine was made according to a recipe for one gallon, and the fermentation was carried out in a completely full demijohn, the resultant wine would be lower in all its constituents by 8%. If the recipe were designed to produce 12% alcohol by volume, the alcohol level would be lowered to 11%. Perhaps the easiest way to allow for this would be to increase all the ingredients by 10%, which would allow the fermentation to be carried out with the gallon jar full. This would be better than conducting the fermentation at a volume of 4.5 litres, leaving an air space, which would encourage contamination and oxidation of the wine.

Another problem encountered is the volume loss when racking the wine from the fermenting jar into a jar of similar size. This volume loss is due to the residual yeast or pulp sediment from the fermentation. In some cases this can be quite substantial, again leading to dilution of the wine if the void space is filled up with water. As it is essential to have the new jar filled to the top and fitted with a suitable airlock, what are the alternatives? Again, allowance could be made for this loss by increasing the amount of the original ingredients. However, this is not suitable as it is hard to predict what these volume losses will be from batch to batch. The best approach, and one used by most experienced winemakers, is to possess a range of jars varying in size from half a gallon up to 5 gallons. When a wine has finished fermentation in a five-gallon jar, it can then be racked into one-gallon and half-gallon demijohns. The sensible winemaker is always on the lookout for suitable fermenting or storage jars. The only stipulation is that they must be made from glass, although one suitable alternative is polycarbonate, which is often used for storing drinking water. The main necessity for the winemaker is to determine the volume that each fermentation vessel will hold, so that recipes can be scaled up or down accordingly.

## Plastic tubing

The tubing is used for siphoning the wine from the fermentation vessel into an empty jar, which is placed at a lower height to achieve the siphoning effect. Plastic is preferable to rubber as it is generally transparent, allowing the level of the liquid in the siphon to be easily seen. The more pliable the tubing the better, the best being silicon rubber tubing. The diameter of the bore of the tubing is best at about 10mm.

## Airlocks

When filled with 10% sodium metabisulphite, airlocks are designed to allow carbon dioxide to escape from the fermenting wine, while preventing air and airborne microbes from entering the fermentation jar.

## Fermentation bin

This is used to carry out pulp fermentation of fruit. The bin should be made of white plastic, and suitable sizes, complete with lids, are 2 gallon and 5 gallon.

## Sieve and funnel

A wire-meshed large sieve and a suitable funnel are indispensable for straining ingredients from the fermentation bin. The juice is strained directly into the fermentation jar in which the rest of the fermentation is completed.

## Bottle brushes

All fermentation jars and wine bottles need to be cleaned and sterilised. The use of sodium metabisulphite for sterilisation is covered in the chapter 'Additives'. Brushes suitable for cleaning all fermentation jars and wine bottles are a necessity. After a vessel has been used, it should be cleaned immediately before the liquid dries out, when ingredients can become encrusted on the glass.

## The hydrometer

The hydrometer is one of the most important pieces of winemaking equipment. Without access to a hydrometer, a winemaker would be struggling to make the correct decisions in some of the steps required to produce a quality wine. The hydrometer measures the specific gravity of liquids. The definition of specific gravity is 'the ratio of the mass of a body to the mass of an equal volume of water at a defined temperature'. In winemaking terms this means the weight of the liquid per unit of volume. Thus a known volume of liquid could be weighed, and the specific gravity calculated. Unfortunately, in order to do this with any degree of accuracy, expensive equipment would be required for both the weighing and the measurement of the volume. The hydrometer allows this measurement of specific gravity with surprising accuracy. The hydrometer is a hollow, weighted, graduated tube. For general winemaking purposes the most common scale is from 0.990-1.150. More accurate measurements can be made with narrower scales such as 0.980-1.000, a scale which would be used for very dry wines. The liquid to be measured is placed in a measuring cylinder or other suitable container, and the reading is taken where the bottom of the meniscus meets the scale. If tap water is put in the measuring cylinder, the reading of the specific gravity should be 1.000, often described as a gravity of 0. Thus a specific gravity reading of 1.040 could also be called a gravity of 40, and one of 0.992 could be called a gravity of -8.

For the winemaker, the hydrometer is effectively measuring the dissolved solids, mainly sugar. Although there are other solids that will be dissolved in the winemaker's must, sugar is by far the most dominant and is the main contributor to the specific gravity reading. It is generally agreed that 1lb sugar in each gallon will produce about 6% alcohol by volume. The average table wine contains about 12% alcohol, requiring 2lbs sugar per gallon. If 2lbs sugar are dissolved in water and made up to 1gallon, the specific gravity reading will be 1.077, although this figure will be higher in a wine must containing 2lbs sugar due to the additional density of the other dissolved substances. The first use of the hydrometer would appear to be for measuring the initial specific gravity of the must in order to produce the required alcohol content. Although this can be done, in practice it is not straightforward, as many of the ingredients may require extraction of juice from solid fruits, and these fruits may not all be added to the fermentation at the same time. Some white wines, and most red wines, make use of fermentations on the pulp, making accurate hydrometer readings of the total sugar content virtually impossible. It is far easier to use tables giving the sugar content of various ingredients, and to calculate the total amount of sugar required to bring the must up to the alcohol level required. Excellent tables giving the sugar content of various fruits and fruit juices are published in *Must* by Gerry Fowles.

By using the relationship between the drop in gravity and the alcohol produced, estimates can be made of the alcohol content of the wine. For this it is best to have all the ingredients in the gallon jar at the start of the fermentation. The initial gravity can then be determined. When fermentation is complete, and the final gravity has been taken, the drop in gravity can be divided by the factor 7.3 to give the alcohol % by volume. Thus each drop in gravity of 7.3 units is equivalent to producing 1% alcohol by volume. The factor 7.3 has been determined by comparing the gravity drop in many wines with the alcohol produced. Although the scale is not linear in that the amount of alcohol produced for each drop of 7.3 gravity units varies slightly depending on the amount of sugar in the must, using a mean figure of 7.3 gives results which realistically compare with the true alcohol values. However, if there is pulp fermentation, or if fruit is being added at different times, this method of calculation is very difficult, being fraught with problems such as volume increases each time an addition is made. Again, estimation of the total sugar content of the must by using tables is a better method.

A more important use of the hydrometer is to monitor the progress of fermentation. If a wine containing 2lbs total sugar in a gallon is monitored daily, a drop in gravity of about 5-10 will be noticed each day, although this drop will slow down with time as the end of fermentation approaches. This slowing down of the rate of fermentation is due to inhibition of the yeast enzymes by the production of alcohol, and by the more limited availability of sugar as it is fermented. If the wine has been designed as a table wine of about 12% alcohol, the wine will be expected to fall to a specific gravity of 0.995-0.990, depending on the other non-fermentable dissolved solids. If a high-alcohol after-dinner wine is being made, requiring a final specific gravity of about 1.040 and as high an alcohol level as possible, the hydrometer is extremely useful in monitoring the specific gravity in order to keep it between 1.020-1.030. This ensures that the highest alcohol level possible under these conditions will be obtained, while still retaining sugar that will help to sweeten the end product. Retention of this sugar in the must avoids reduction of the alcohol content due to the addition of extra sugar, which would increase the volume. Similarly, if a high-alcohol, dry-aperitif style was desired, monitoring of the sugar content would be performed in order to keep the specific gravity just under 1.000, finally allowing the wine to ferment out to complete dryness.

The last, but certainly not least, use of the hydrometer is to sweeten finished wines. Unless stabilisers are added, few wines remain stable for long periods of time once they have been sweetened. The hydrometer is tremendously helpful when sweetening wines shortly before they are required. For example, suppose a gallon of a heavy-bodied, sweet, white wine has been allowed to ferment out to specific gravity 0.990, and it needs to be sweetened for a show in a week's time. Such a wine will probably drink best at a specific gravity of about 1.030. The best way is to take a litre of the wine and sweeten it to 1.050, a level of sweetness that obviously will be too high for the style. Blends of the dry version and the sweet version can easily be made in order to decide the optimum degree of sweetness for this particular wine. Equal portions of each will give about 1.020, two of sweet to one of dry will give about 1.030, and five of sweet to two of dry will give about 1.033. Further tasting and honing around these levels of sweetness will give the balance required in the wine. At this stage, the acidity can be adjusted if required. If necessary, the whole batch can then be sweetened to the same level. If only a portion of the wine is to be sweetened, the remainder of the dry wine can be stored in smaller vessels or bottles until required. As the correct level of sweetness will have already been decided, the wine can then be sweetened to the pre-determined specific gravity.

# three
# HOW WINE IS MADE

# How Wine is Made

Wine is made by the conversion of sugar to alcohol. Grape juice, which contains about 20% sugar and no alcohol, is converted to wine containing about 12% alcohol and no sugar. A cascade of enzymes, which are secreted by the yeast cells, achieves the fermentation of the sugar to alcohol. Over a series of sequential reactions, these enzymes convert the 6-carbon sugars, glucose and fructose, into the 2-carbon alcohol molecule ethanol. Carbon dioxide is also produced, being released as bubbles, which can be used as a measure of the rate of fermentation. When making a wine, the amateur winemaker is attempting to mimic this procedure using either grapes, concentrates produced from grapes, indigenous fruits, fruit juices, or suitable blends of these. During the process of fermentation, other important taste constituents of the grape, such as acid and tannin, remain fairly stable.

Before examining how amateur wine is made in the home, first look at the commercial scene. Although commercial wine is made in very large batches, the volume of wine produced from the grapes used works out to about 1 gallon of wine for every 14lbs of grapes. The serendipity that has been endowed upon the grape is such that the balance of the ingredients making up the grape juice is ideal for winemaking. The main tastes involved in the final balance of a wine are sugar, alcohol, acidity, and tannin. These constituents fine-tune the actual flavour of the wine that comes from the grape variety used. If the alcohol is too low, the wine will taste thin and watery, while it will be hot on the palate and in the aftertaste if the alcohol content is too high. Low acidity will give a somewhat flabby wine, and the wine will taste cringingly tart if the acidity is too high. Sugar and tannin influence these two tastes. Tannin tastes more astringent as the alcohol increases. The sweeter a wine is, the more acidity it can have. These four tastes are all linked, and compliment each other in the best wines.

How does this compare with the amateur scene where the winemaker is attempting to make a wine similar to the commercial style, but with ingredients other than grapes? Examining the balance of the grape first, grapes have about 0.6% acid when measured as tartaric acid (i.e., if all the acids there were tartaric acid, 0.6% would be the value: all acidity quotes in this book will use tartaric as the standard acid). The sugar content of grapes can vary, but most well-ripened grapes contain at least 20% sugar, capable of producing over 12% alcohol by volume. Most of the tannin in grapes is situated on the skins, the quickly-expressed juice having only a fraction of the total. Typical values for the tannin content of grape skins are 1.5%-2.0%. Consider the amateur winemaker making a red wine from grapes with these values. As the free-run grape juice from most red grapes is colourless, a fermentation on the pulp will be necessary in order to extract the colour and tannin from the grape skins. In making a gallon of wine, about 14lbs grapes will be required. The grapes must be crushed without breaking the pips, as this would release unwanted bitterness into the wine. The crushed grapes are then inoculated with a good wine yeast and the fermentation is carried out in a suitable fermentation bin with periodic stirring. After a suitable length of time, normally about four days, the juice will be strained into a gallon jar, and fermented to dryness. If the grapes are of good quality, the resultant wine should have an alcohol content of about 12%, an acidity of about 0.6%, and a tannin level of about 0.2%. The wine should look, smell, and taste like its commercial counterpart.

The making of that wine from grapes required 14lbs fruit. If the amateur made a gallon of wine from 14lbs elderberries with no other additions, how would it compare to the wine made from grapes? It would have just over half the alcohol content, about twice as much acid, and about four times as much tannin. Imagine the taste! The reason for this is that the same weight of elderberries contain about half as much sugar and twice as much acid as the same weight of grapes. Additionally, when the diameter of an elderberry is compared with the diameter of a grape, the diameter of the elderberry is about a fourth of that of the grape. As readers will remember from their schoolchild mathematics, this means that, in equal weights of elderberries and grapes, there is four times as much elderberry skin as there is grape skin, and hence the reason for the high tannin value in the gallon of elderberry wine. Similarly, if a white wine were made solely from gooseberry juice, it would be about three times too high in acid and three times too low in alcohol when compared to a wine made from white grape juice. Clearly, it is not that simple to make wine from fruits other than grapes.

There have been many books on home-made wine over the years, but it was not until the works of Bryan Acton and Peter Duncan in the 1960s that amateur winemaking was brought into the modern era with the introduction of sensible scientific information that led to the design of excellent recipes that could help the winemaker to make wines similar to the commercial styles. Two of their books, *Making Wines Like Those You Buy* and *Progressive Winemaking*, have stood the test of time, and should be on every winemaker's bookshelf. More recently, Professor Gerry Fowles has expanded in great depth our knowledge of all aspects associated not only with home winemaking, but also with how the technology used in the commercial scene can be incorporated into the amateur world. Again, no winemaker should be without Gerry's books *Must* and *Winemaking in Style*. Before these authors appeared on the scene, it was not unusual to find recipes with high sugar additions inappropriate to the style of wine that would be produced from the fruits used. Imagine a recipe for one gallon of wine with the following ingredients:

| | |
|---|---|
| Raspberries | 5lbs |
| Redcurrants | 3lbs |
| Sugar | 4lbs |
| Nutrients | |
| Yeast | |

These are the ingredients for 1 gallon of wine. As the fruit will contain about 8oz sugar, the potential alcohol from the sugar in the must is about 27% (by volume). Obviously the wine would never ferment out, and probably stop about 18% alcohol, leaving a high-alcohol, rosé-coloured wine, with a residual specific gravity of around 1.050, which is at least as high as most dessert-style wines. Without taking into consideration any acidity produced during the fermentation, the acidity in the fruit alone would give a final acidity of 1.5%, which is more than twice the amount found in even the highest-acidity wines. Again, imagine the taste!

Thankfully, we have marched on from such recipes. The information supplied by the authors above allows us to design our own recipes, so that they will have the correct amounts of initial sugar, acid, and tannin to produce the style of wine required. All that remains to be done is to select sensible blends of fruits, fruit juices, and concentrates to give the required flavours. Much in the way of recipe design can be learned from the cook. Over the years, tried and trusted recipes have produced desserts where the fruits used complement each other. For example, rhubarb and strawberry go together, as do apple and blackberry. Gooseberry and apple would not be a good match, and neither would rhubarb and redcurrant. Inevitably, I find that those blends that work for the cook also work for the winemaker. Let us examine how a simple recipe might be designed and then look at how the same recipe might be improved. However, we should first change the percentage figures for final alcohol, acidity, and tannin into the required amounts of sugar, acid, and tannin required in the ingredients which will make up the must. 12% alcohol will require 32oz sugar in 4.5 litres (1 gallon), 0.5% acid will require 22.5g acid in 4.5 litres, and 0.2% tannin will require 9.0g tannin in 4.5 litres.

We have seen that its constituents make elderberry unsuitable to be used alone to make wine, as the acidity and tannin are high, and the sugar is low. If a wine has to be made only from elderberries which have a tannin content of about 0.5% (all information such as this has been taken from *Must* by Gerry Fowles), then 4lbs elderberries per gallon of wine is as high as we would want to go, giving a tannin content in the completed wine of about 0.2% (9g). The 4lbs elderberries would contain about 6oz sugar and would give a final acidity in a gallon of 0.4% (18g). If there are no other ingredients other than yeast and nutrients, the total sugar content needs raising to 32oz, and the total acidity needs raising to 0.5%, a rise of about 0.1%, which would require the addition of 4.5g tartaric acid. The design of the recipe would then be:

| | Sugar | Acid | Tannin |
|---|---|---|---|
| Elderberries | 64oz | 6oz | 18g | 9g |
| Sugar | 26oz | 26oz | | |
| Tartaric acid | 4.5g | | 4.5g | |
| Total | | 32oz | 22.5g | 9g |

Of course, the recipe would also have other additives such as nutrients, pectolase, and yeast, but I have omitted these in order to simplify the recipe table. When complete, this wine is now in the right ball park for a dry red table wine. It should be bone dry, with a good balance of alcohol (12% by volume), acidity (0.5%), and tannin (0.2%). However, the taste may be too weighted on elderberry, and may lack the complexity of good quality red wines. Other red fruits could be introduced into the recipe in place of some of the elderberry, and some of the sugar and acidity required could be obtained from red grape concentrate. Below is a recipe where blackberry has been introduced to replace some of the elderberry, and grape concentrate has been introduced to provide sugar, acidity, body, and vinosity, the latter term being used to describe the taste and texture associated with wines made from grapes. The acidity, sugar, and tannin values shown can all be found in *Must*. The amounts shown are the amounts that each ingredient will contribute to a gallon of wine.

| | Sugar | Acid | Tannin |
|---|---|---|---|
| Elderberries | 32oz | 3oz | 9.0g | 4.6g |
| Blackberries | 16oz | 1oz | 4.5g | 2.3g |
| Red grape concentrate | 10fl oz | 8oz | 5.6g | 2.0g* |
| Sugar | 20oz | 20oz | | |
| Tartaric acid | 4.0g | | 4.0g | |
| Total | | 32oz | 23.1g | 8.9g |

* The tannin value for the grape concentrate is an estimate as there is much variation in the brands available, and there is little published information.

If we tasted this wine against the wine made only from elderberries, we would find that it was more interesting and more complex than the elderberry wine, yet they have the same amount of alcohol, acid, and tannin. The wine can be further improved by the addition of oak granules during the pulp fermentation, and by the addition of small amounts of highly-flavoured fruits such as raspberry and lychee. By using small amounts of these fruits, of the order of 2oz each, the bouquet and flavour are improved without significant changes to the alcohol, acid, and tannin. The final recipe, complete with instructions, is shown below in both imperial and metric units.

| | | |
|---|---|---|
| Red grape concentrate | 16fl oz | 454g |
| Elderberries | 32oz | 907g |
| Blackberries | 16oz | 454g |
| Raspberries | 2oz | 57g |
| Lychee flesh | 2oz | 57g |
| Sugar | 20oz | 567g |
| Oak granules | 1oz | 28g |
| Nutrients | | |
| Pectolase | | |
| Yeast, Gervin no. 3 | | |

Dilute the grape concentrate and nutrients in 4 pints of water, and use it to build up the yeast culture over a period of 4 days. At this stage, pasteurise the elderberries and blackberries in a pot by barely covering them with water and heating just to boiling. Cool immediately, mash, and treat with pectolase according to manufacturer's instructions. Transfer to a fermentation bin, adding the sugar, oak, and the yeast starter. Make sure that the sugar is totally dissolved, and ferment on the pulp for 4 days. Stir often to break the cap that will be formed on top of the must. After the 4-day pulp fermentation, add the pasteurised, mashed raspberry and lychee, and ferment on the pulp for a further 4 hours, stirring occasionally. Rack into a gallon jar, top up with water, and ferment to dryness, which should be a specific gravity of between 0.990 and 0.995. Rack, and fine as necessary. Bottle when clear.

I have not given amounts of nutrients, pectolase, or yeast, as these should be used as suggested by the manufacturer. The reasons for adding some of the fruit much later in the fermentation will be explained in the chapter 'Ingredients and How to Use Them'.

This recipe will produce wine capable of winning prizes at shows. The build-up from a basic elderberry wine shows that it is not difficult to design recipes from the fruits available for winemaking. As discussed earlier, fruits that complement each other in taste will blend together well in wine. Surprisingly, the more ingredients there are in a wine the more reproducible the wine is. This is because seasonal variations in only one ingredient have less overall effect in a wine that is made from more than one ingredient.

The wine that has been developed above is a dry red table wine, only one of many different wine styles. For the other wine styles, the alcohol, acidity, and tannin will vary as shown in the selection below. The figures have been obtained from *Must* by Gerry Fowles.

| | Alcohol | Acidity | Tannin |
|---|---|---|---|
| | (% by volume) | (% tartaric) | (%) |
| Dry White Table | 9-13 | 0.55-0.70 | <0.04 |
| Dry Red Table | 11-13 | 0.50-0.65 | 0.1-0.3 |
| Sweet White Table | 8-15 | 0.50-0.75 | <0.04 |
| After-dinner Red | 17-20 | 0.55-0.65 | 0.2-0.3 |

The values given for the acidity are the values required in the completed wine. Acid is produced during the fermentation, typically a rise of about 0.15%. Therefore, the acidity in the initial must should be reduced accordingly, or adjusted in the final wine as described in the chapter 'Winemaking Additives'.

# four
# WINEMAKING ADDITIVES

The additives discussed here are those that would normally be added along with the fruit ingredients at the start of the fermentation, or very early in the fermentation. Other ingredients used for clarifying the completed wine are described in the chapter 'From Racking to Bottling'.

### Yeast starter

This has to be the most important additive, without which it is doubtful if any decent fermentation would be initiated. In the past, home winemakers had limited availability to wine yeasts, relying on baker's yeast or the wild strains on the fruits that they used. Modern winemakers are fortunate in having a range of commercially derived pure wine yeasts to use in their fermentations. Different strains of these yeasts can be used to make different styles of wine. For example, there are yeasts that are capable of producing high alcohol levels, necessary for most after-dinner style wines. All these yeasts are available as dried yeasts which are revived after about half an hour in water at about 30°C. At this stage, the best method to prime the yeast (i.e., to stimulate it into rapid multiplication) is to keep doubling its volume every hour with white grape juice, until there is a volume of at least a pint. More information on the building up of the yeast starter is given in the chapter 'Ingredients and How to Use Them'.

### Metabisulphite

Sulphiting is the name given to treatment with sodium or potassium metabisulphite. Metabisulphite reacts with dissolved oxygen in the must to produce an anaerobic environment in which few of the contaminants we find in winemaking can survive, although under these anaerobic conditions the yeast will produce alcohol. In addition, when the metabisulphite dissolves, it releases free sulphur dioxide, which has bactericidal, and fungicidal action. Indeed, the scavenging of oxygen and the biocidal effects are the two main uses of metabisulphite by the amateur. These uses of metabisulphite take place at three different stages of the winemaking process, the sterilisation of equipment before fermentation, the sterilisation of ingredients, and the racking and maturing of the wine after fermentation is complete. If we examine these three stages separately, the first is to sterilise equipment such as gallon jars, fermentation bins, and bottles. Making up a 10% solution of metabisulphite, and using this to rinse out the containers best does this. If all the internal surface of the container is wetted with the metabisulphite solution, a few minutes will be sufficient to achieve sterilisation. The container should be washed well with water immediately and inverted to drain. Care should be taken to do most of the manipulations outdoors, and to avoid breathing any released sulphur dioxide. Stored in a bottle with minimal air space, a 10% solution of metabisulphite will remain potent for many months. This solution, or a more dilute 1% solution, can also be used for swabbing benches and the outsides of vessels used in winemaking.

The second use of metabisulphite is to sterilise fruit and other ingredients, especially those whose flavours would be impaired by heat treatment. The recommended doses are between 5 and 10ml of a 10% solution of metabisulphite per gallon of liquid. These amounts give final concentrations of metabisulphite of 100 parts per million (ppm) to 200ppm, with available sulphur dioxide levels of just over half these values. Metabisulphite is also available as Campden tablets, one tablet per gallon giving a metabisulphite concentration of 100ppm. At doses of 100-200ppm, metabisulphite has the selective ability to inhibit contaminating wild yeasts and bacteria without lowering the activity of the true wine yeasts. Another way to consider why these amounts are used is to consider the amounts of oxygen encountered in a normal fermentation. At normal room temperatures of around 20°C, there are about 45mg oxygen dissolved in each gallon of tap water, equivalent to just over 30ml oxygen. Adding metabisulphite to a final concentration of 100ppm will neutralise all the dissolved oxygen in a gallon of fresh water. Thus, the addition of the metabisulphite should be enough to produce an anaerobic environment in which few contaminating organisms will survive, as most of these organisms require oxygen as part of their energy source. As already mentioned, the metabisulphite will also produce free sulphur dioxide which has the added advantage of possessing a bactericidal effect. But are these levels of metabisulphite really needed in order to achieve the aim of the winemaker, which is surely to start the fermentation so that only the required yeast strain is multiplying in the wine must? I think not. If we look at the make up of many amateur non-grape recipes, there are about 4lbs of fruit, some grape concentrate, sugar, and a lot of water. For example, consider a recipe with 2lbs fresh gooseberry, 1 litre fresh pressed apple juice, 10fl oz white grape concentrate, and 16oz sugar, designed for one gallon. Over 50% of the final volume will have come from added water, but why treat this water with metabisulphite? By boiling and cooling, the added water can be sterilised, while at the same time the process will reduce the dissolved oxygen content. However, I do not think that this is necessary as the standard of our tap water is very high, and any minor contamination that does exist will be swamped by a strong yeast inoculum as will be explained. In addition, the oxygen dissolved in the water is advantageous initially in helping to build up a yeast colony very fast, as the energy obtained by the yeast in the presence of oxygen is over ten times that obtained under anaerobic conditions. Of the ingredients above, the only ones that need metabisulphite treatment are the gooseberries and the apple juice. As the total volume of the crushed gooseberries and the apple juice will be about 2 litres, these ingredients can be sterilised with metabisulphite to a final concentration of 100ppm, requiring less than half the amount that would be used if the must was made up to 1 gallon at this stage. As described in the chapter 'Ingredients and How to Use Them', the yeast starter would have already been initiated with the grape concentrate and sugar in a volume of about 2 litres. Ideally, this would have been started about a week ahead of the processing of the gooseberries and apples. After overnight sterilisation with metabisulphite, the free-run juice from the gooseberry and apple can be added to the yeast starter, or, if preferred, a pulp fermentation can be carried out. Handling fermentations in this way guarantees that the selected yeast strain will at no time have to compete with well-established amounts of contaminating organisms, while, at the same time, sulphur levels are reduced to a more desirable level. After all, the less metabisulphite that is added to a wine during its making, the less sulphur there will be in the final bottle of wine.

The third main use of metabisulphite is during the racking and maturing stages. When a wine has finished fermentation, it will be saturated with carbon dioxide, with virtually no dissolved oxygen in the wine or in the space between the wine and the airlock. The airlock should be filled with 10% metabisulphite. When most of the solids have settled, assuming that the fermentation has been conducted in a gallon jar, the wine should be siphoned into another gallon jar, but very carefully. The requirement here is to siphon the wine with as little air contact as possible. The end of the siphon tube going into the empty gallon jar should be placed on the bottom of the jar, and the wine siphoned with as little turbulence as possible. The dissolving of oxygen from the air into wine at this stage is increased dramatically by vortex effects caused by stirring and turbulence. By avoiding these vortex effects, the wine can retain much of its dissolved carbon dioxide instead of replacing it with air, of which 21% will be oxygen. When the wine has been safely transferred to the new gallon jar, there will be an air space due to the solids left behind in the other jar. This should be topped up immediately with either wine of a similar style or water that has been boiled and cooled. It is at this stage that standard procedures require the addition of 100-200ppm metabisulphite. Again, I query, is this amount really necessary? If the wine has been racked carefully and the jar has been topped up close to the airlock, there will be little dissolved oxygen in the wine in the jar. The amounts of metabisulphite mentioned above are way in excess of what is required to neutralise any small amounts of dissolved oxygen. The other problem of oxygen-dependent organisms growing on the surface of the wine can easily be eliminated by slowly layering 1-2ml 10% metabisulphite on the top of the wine leaving as little space as possible between this and the airlock. This gives a gradient of concentration of sodium metabisulphite, with the highest concentration at the top of the jar where it is most needed. The wine is now properly sealed from the air, and has been rendered oxygen free without the winemaker being heavy handed on the use of metabisulphite. In the making of sparkling wine, winemakers should be very sparing in the use of metabisulphite, especially during the racking of the first fermentation. As the environment in a totally-sealed sparkling wine bottle will be oxygen free, the pungent odour of sulphur dioxide will remain in the wine.

The racked wine should be left in a cool area to allow further settling of solids. When no further clearing of the wine is occurring, the wine should be racked again, taking the same precautions as in the previous racking. At this stage the wine should be fined with the winemaker's choice of fining agent, taking great care to stir the finings into the wine very slowly to keep any oxygen absorption as low as possible. Again, a small addition of metabisulphite on the top of the wine should be sufficient. When clear, one more racking under the same conditions should be sufficient to give a clear wine with minimal dissolved oxygen and lower sulphur content than by standard recommended protocols. Improved cleanliness in winemaking techniques has lowered the amounts of sulphite used in the commercial world. Heeding the advice above can achieve the same goals in the amateur field.

## Pectolase treatment

Virtually all the fruits and other ingredients we use in winemaking contain pectin which, if not removed, may cause hazes in the wine, even after racking and fining. The best way to avoid the resultant haze due to pectin is to treat the fruit with the enzyme pectolase (often described as pectolytic enzyme) early in the fermentation. Pectolase will break down the pectin to smaller molecules, which are totally soluble in the wine. As pectolase, like all enzymes, works better when its substrate, pectin, is in higher concentrations, it pays to treat only the ingredients requiring treatment before they are added to the must. Thus, if a gallon of wine is being made from 2 litres supermarket white grape juice and 4lbs gooseberries, only the gooseberries need to be mashed and treated with pectolase. Most supermarket white grape juice is clear and does not require treatment. By treating the gooseberries before they are diluted with water, the action of the pectolase is more efficient. As pectolase works equally as well in anaerobic conditions, the enzyme treatment can be carried out at the same time as the metabisulphite treatment of the fruit. Some commercial fruit juices, such as fresh pressed apple juice and orange juice, are cloudy and will require treatment. The best rule of thumb is to treat all solid fruits and any juice that is not clear.

## Nutrients

In order to survive, yeast requires sources of carbon, nitrogen, phosphorus, minerals, trace elements, and vitamins. The carbon source is sugar, either as added sucrose or as the sugars already present in the fruits used. In a wine made solely from fully-ripened grapes, there will be sufficient sugar in the must to produce a wine with the required alcohol level. In addition, there is usually sufficient of the other nutrients mentioned to sustain adequate growth of the yeast. Most of the fruits used in amateur winemaking have lower levels of sugar than the grape, and have varying amounts of the other nutrients. However, in more complex recipes requiring two or more different fruits, there are usually sufficient amounts of the necessary nutrients to carry out the fermentation successfully. The required amount of sugar can be calculated and added. In recipes with a mixture of fruits, a good suggestion is to add about half the recommended amounts of ammonium phosphate and other nutrients. The best source of these is the Gervin product Minavit that contains balanced amounts of nitrogen, phosphorus, minerals, trace elements, and vitamins. Where a wine is being made from minimal ingredients, for example a flower wine with little or no fruit, nutrients will be essential for the fermentation to be conducted successfully. Of course, such a wine will also need to have the addition of the required amounts of sugar and acid. Extra amounts of nutrients are needed to produce high-alcohol wines. A booklet on the use of Gervin products is available from the manufacturer.

## Bentonite

Bentonite, usually available as a grey powder, is a diatomaceous earth, which swells when mixed with water. It has a large adsorptive capacity, and is best made as a 5% slurry in water by mixing it with a little water at a time as one would to make gravy. Any lumps should be sieved out before use. Bentonite works best on white wines, where it should be incorporated into the fermentation as early as possible, at a level of about 50ml of the 5% suspension per gallon of wine. In addition to removing protein hazes, it results in very smooth fermentations, often leaving the wine remarkably clear before the first racking, especially when used on wines which have not been pulp fermented.

**Acid**

Few wines made by the amateur winemaker will suffer from low-acidity, as most of the fruits used have much higher acidity levels than the grape. The low acidity wines likely to be made are those using ingredients such as flowers and vine prunings. It is necessary to adjust low-acidity wines at the start of the fermentation, as high acidity in the wine helps to lower contamination problems. The yeast can perform well under high acidity while most bacteria find such conditions quite hostile. Required acidity levels are given in the chapter 'How Wine Is Made', and adjustments can be made by the addition of the appropriate amount of acid. The two most common acids used for this purpose are citric acid and tartaric acid. Tartaric acid has the advantage that it is not readily metabolised by contaminating organisms. However, tartaric acid will crystallise out when stored at low temperatures. Hence, it can be described as an advantage or disadvantage. On the other hand, citric acid will stay in solution, but can be used as an energy source by bacteria, producing undesirable off flavours in the process. As there are advocates for both these acids, I leave it to the winemaker to make the choice. One level teaspoon of these acids to a gallon of wine will raise the acidity of the wine by about 0.1%, an increase of around 20% for most low-acid wines.

Where wines are too acidic, the acidity can be reduced either early in the fermentation or when the wine is clarified. The two most common salts used to reduce acidity are calcium carbonate (chalk) and potassium hydrogen carbonate (potassium bicarbonate). Calcium carbonate is best used early in the fermentation, especially during any pulp fermentation, while potassium hydrogen carbonate is best used on the clarified wine. About one level teaspoon of potassium hydrogen carbonate or half a level teaspoon of calcium carbonate will reduce the acidity of a gallon of wine by about 0.1%.

How is the acidity determined? To do this accurately requires titration i.e., estimating the amount of a standard alkaline solution required to neutralise a set volume of wine. The average winemaker does not normally carry this out, as a certain amount of laboratory skill and equipment is required. If titration is not carried out, the acidity in the wine can be estimated fairly accurately by using the acidity tables to be found in *Must* by Gerry Fowles. However, in the final judgement of the completed wine, the best estimate of the level of acidity will be made by the winemaker's palate.

# five
# FROM RACKING
# TO BOTTLING

When fermentation has ceased, as shown by the lack of production of bubbles of carbon dioxide rising to the surface of the wine, the wine needs to be stabilised and clarified. As soon as there is a firm deposit on the bottom of the gallon jar, the wine should be siphoned into another jar of similar size. This is best achieved by using pliable tubing with an internal bore of about 10mm. Silicone rubber tubing is best if you can find some. During this manipulation, great care should be taken to ensure that there is as little splashing as possible, as splashing and the creating of vortex effects cause the wine to absorb oxygen. When the wine has finished fermentation, there will be virtually no dissolved oxygen in the wine. Therefore, by keeping the gallon jar filled to as near the brim as possible, and by avoiding unnecessary splashing, the wine can be kept as close to an anaerobic condition as possible. There will be a volume loss in racking due to the space occupied by the settled yeast and any pulp from the fruit, leading to an air space in the jar into which the wine has been racked. This air space can be filled with water, which has been boiled and cooled. However, with two rackings for each wine, this volume loss creeps up to around 10%. If the wine is topped up with water, then all the constituents of the wine will be reduced by about 10%. One way to offset this is to increase the amounts of the ingredients used to allow for this loss of volume during racking. When working solely with one-gallon batches of wine, another method is to top up the air space due to racking with wine of a similar style, eliminating any dilution of the alcohol or other qualities of the wine. One enterprising winemaker I know adds marbles to eliminate the air space! However, especially with tried and trusted recipes, the best method is to make larger quantities of wine, say five gallons at a time. At the time of racking, the wine can then be racked from the five-gallon container into one-gallon jars, the last gallon being distributed into one-litre bottles. This method always leaves enough for a little taste for the winemaker! The gallon jars should be filled as close to the fitted airlock as possible.

Oxygen absorption can also be controlled by the addition of metabisulphite after the wine has been racked, 5ml of a 10% solution being the generally accepted amount. This has been discussed in the chapter 'Additives', where it was indicated that lower amounts of metabisulphite could be used if the rackings are carried out carefully, and the gallon jars kept full to the brim. It was also suggested that any metabisulphite additions be on the top of the wine, thus initially forming a gradient with the highest concentration where it is most needed. The less metabisulphite that is added to the wine the less there will be in the end product. Depending on the ingredients that have been used, the wine may need one more racking before the fining process. With some wines, especially with white wines where bentonite has been used, the wines will fall clear without the need for fining or filtering.

When the wine shows no more signs of clearing on its own, it should be fined. There is a selection of commercial fining agents available using the binding properties of products such as chitin, isinglass, silicic acid, gelatine, and bentonite. Silicic acid and gelatine are usually supplied as a two-part fining agent, and in my experience have proven to be the best products for the clarification of wines. Chitin and isinglass appear to be more selective, only working on some batches of wine. These reagents should be used according to manufacturers' instructions, which usually suggest storing the wine in a cool environment once the fining agent has been mixed into the wine. When used at the start of non-pulp fermentations of white wine, bentonite is efficient in eliminating protein hazes. When clear, the wine should be racked carefully, and topped up using one of the methods already discussed, again leaving a minimal airspace between the wine and the airlock. More details on the use of these fining agents are available in the section 'Hazes' in the chapter 'When Things Go Wrong'.

Occasionally, one runs across a wine that does not respond completely to fining, leaving a haze in the wine. If pectolase has been used correctly during the fruit processing, then pectin is unlikely to be the cause, which was almost certainly a poor choice of ingredients. At this stage the wine should be filtered, using one of the commercially available filtration kits. Most of these work on two filtration pads clamped together in a sealed unit. The wine is pumped through using a hand pump. As these filters, once set up, can process five to ten gallons of wine before clogging up, they are only worth using for large batches of wine. Alternatively, invite some friends round to filter their wine also. One point to note is that the filters need extensive soaking in water before use to remove cellulose taints, which are extremely detrimental to wine. After soaking, a gallon of water needs to be pumped through followed by a pint of an indifferent clean wine. The wine can then be filtered, care being taken to avoid splashing of the wine and any excess exposure to the air. Although filtration should be regarded as a last resort, I am very keen to have my white wines crystal clear as soon as possible. This always reassures me that I have no contamination problems. With a cloudy wine, problems could exist.

White wines, as soon as they are crystal clear and show no more signs of throwing any deposit, should be bottled and sealed with straight corks. These wines can then benefit from lengths of storage from three months onwards. Most red wines benefit from further oak maturation. Methods of oak maturation for the amateur are discussed in the chapter 'Oak', but at this stage, where the wine has been clarified and is stable, the best method is to put two strips of new oak in a gallon of wine for at least six months. Ideally a five-gallon batch of wine would have been racked during clarification into smaller vessels, some of which could be oaked, and some of which could be unoaked. The oaked and unoaked could then be compared at three monthly intervals. When the red wines have been suitably matured, they can be bottled and stored for periods of six months to many years depending on their style. All bottled wines should be fitted with a plastic sleeve over the cork, and should be suitably labelled before storage. So much more is added to the presentation of a bottle of wine when it looks like its commercial cousin rather than a bottle on which a scrap of label bears some faded scribble.

# six
# INGREDIENTS AND HOW TO USE THEM

The most important decision in making a wine is undoubtedly the choice of ingredients that will constitute the recipe. The first step, of course, will be to design the recipe so that a good balance of the fruits is achieved. The recipe needs to have the correct amounts of sugar and fruit acids to achieve the final alcohol and acidity levels required for good balance, with quality coming from a blend of suitable fruits chosen so that they complement each other. One way to help to select fruits on the basis of their compatibility is discussed in the chapter 'Recipe Design'. Assuming that the recipe has already been designed and that the method of preparing the chosen fruits has been decided, this chapter will discuss the possibilities of using the fruits wisely by judicious timing of their addition to the fermentation. However, initially, the best methods of fruit extraction and sterilisation will be examined, with white fruits and red fruits being discussed separately, as there is a greater need for pulp fermentation with red fruits.

## White fruit juices

Excellent ingredients for making white wines are fruit juices available in supermarkets, covering a wide range of fruits such as grape, apple, and peach to mixes of more exotic fruits such as mango and guava. These are ideal for winemaking, but the more aromatic fruit juices should only be used in small proportions to blend with more traditional juices. One great advantage of these juices, usually packaged in one-litre cartons, is that they are sterile and do not require treatment with sodium metabisulphite.

## White fruit

It is generally agreed by winemakers that the best white wines are made from the extracted juices of fruits rather than from pulp fermentation of crushed fruit, thus avoiding prolonged contact with the fruit skins and, hence, the extraction of harsh astringent flavours unsuitable for white-wine styles. The best examples of this principle are commercial white wines which are made from the juice run off from the first pressings of the grapes. If any skin contact is allowed at all in commercial white wine-making, it tends to be minimal and occurs before the grape juice is separated from the solids. Therefore, if fresh grapes are being used, they should be crushed just enough to break the skins before straining off the juice. This can be done using a commercial crusher, although a potato masher is very effective for small quantities. As soon as the fruit is crushed, it should be treated with metabisulphite, enough to keep the juice at 100ppm (parts per million), equivalent to 0.01%. This is best done by making up a 10% solution of sodium metabisulphite, and adding 1ml to every litre of pulp (1 teaspoon to every gallon). If some skin contact is required, the crushed fruit can be left overnight before straining to give the required juice. This is an appropriate time to treat with pectolase, the addition being to manufacturer's instructions. A light pressing is required to give a higher yield of juice. More juice can be extracted by heavier pressing, but this is of lesser quality and is best processed separately. Any shrewd winemaker will, of course, find a good use for the pulp in some heavier wine style. The extracted juice can then be fermented on its own or blended with other ingredients depending on the recipe design. Later in this chapter, advice on the yeast starter used will be given and should be followed.

Other soft white fruit such as gooseberries should be treated similarly to the method used for processing white grapes, although some of these fruits are better when pre-frozen in order to break down the fruit cells, thus releasing the juice more easily. Rhubarb should be chopped and frozen in chunks before use. Just covering with cold sulphited water should thaw the rhubarb. When thawed, pectolase should be added for 4 hours, and the juice strained with a very light pressing. Among a variety of methods available for hard fruits such as apples, pears, and peaches are steam extraction, vacuum extraction, the use of fruit presses and centrifugal juice extractors, and diffusion from the thinly-sliced fruit. The latter of these, diffusion, is a speedy and efficient way of dealing with these fruits but needs 24 hours for a good extraction of juice, resulting in excessive skin and pulp contact which can lead to harshness and astringency in the final wines. Steam, vacuum, and centrifugal extraction are efficient but only lend themselves to small-scale production. A fruit press is the ideal machine but often is not readily available to the winemaker. Whichever method is used, the fruit still needs to be sterilised with metabisulphite. Often, however, these extracts only make up a small proportion of the total wine volume, the other ingredients being, say, grape concentrate and water. In this case, only the juice extracted from the fruits needs to be sterilised, thus cutting down on the total metabisulphite used and leading to a faster fermentation with less residual sulphur in the completed wine. This also applies to pectolase treatment, which is not required on some of the ingredients such as grape juice and other clarified juices. This means that only a small percentage of the total volume needs to be treated with pectolase, a distinct advantage since enzymes perform better in higher concentrations of their substrates. The extracted juices can then be combined and fermentation started, but do note that the necessity for a sensible size of yeast inoculum is considered later in this chapter.

### White fruit concentrates

These cover grape concentrates, fruit concentrates, and mixtures of both. In general, the use of these concentrates is to be avoided in lighter-style wines, and they should be reserved for sherry-style wines, heavy, sweet wines, and after-dinner wines. The reason for this is that they tend to be caramelised, giving the finished wine an undesirable brown colour and oxidised characteristics. The fruit concentrates often have the addition of artificial flavourings, which can be detected in the end product. However, their use in dessert-style wines is to be encouraged, not only as an ingredient in the must, but also as a method of sweetening the wine as discussed in the chapter 'A Versatile Wine'.

### Red fruit juices

In general, these should be avoided, since artificial colouring has been added due to the difficulty in extracting colour from the skins of the fruits used to make the red fruit juices. These colour additions seldom look natural, are often unstable, and are prone to precipitation in the final wine.

### Red fruit

The treatment of red fruit for making red wine takes on a completely different complexion from the treatments described above for white fruit in the making of white wine. Whereas pulp fermentation was to be discouraged with white fruit, pulp fermentation is mandatory in the making of quality red wine. Commercially, grapes are crushed and, depending on the grape and style of wine to be produced, fermented on the pulp for 2-30 days in order to release the colour pigments and tannins, these being more readily solubilised as the alcohol content rises.

In amateur winemaking, grapes and soft red fruits can be crushed and treated with metabisulphite and pectolase as for the white fruits. With some red fruits such as elderberries, the bacterial and wild yeast contamination can be very high, requiring pasteurisation rather than sulphite sterilisation. Here the fruit needs to be taken to just below boiling point and held above 80°C for ten minutes, followed by instant cooling. This will kill all surviving organisms except spores, which will not cause a problem provided the fermentation is carried out smartly. When the fruit has cooled, it is best crushed with a potato masher, treated with pectolase, and put straight into a suitable container for the pulp fermentation. Later in this chapter the best timing for this pulp fermentation will be revealed. Most of the red fruits can be handled in this way, giving good flavour, colour, and tannin extractions during the pulp fermentation. It is best to avoid liquidisers as they break the pips, releasing excess astringency and bitterness.

### Red fruit concentrates

Again, these consist of grape concentrates, fruit concentrates, and mixtures of both. They are very good for making amateur wines, with sensible blends of concentrates and red fruits making excellent amateur wines, particularly heavy sweet and after-dinner styles.

This has been a brief summary of the general methods for the handling of fruits, juices, and concentrates for making various wine styles. Individual fruits have been discussed in more detail by Gerry Fowles in Winemaking in Style and by Acton and Duncan in Progressive Winemaking. What needs to be considered now is how to get the best mileage from the treated ingredients used to formulate the recipe.

## How to get the best mileage from the fruit

Imagine Joe, our average club winemaker, deciding to make a wine in the autumn. Seeing elderberries everywhere, he picks them, takes them home, separates fruit from stalks, and then looks for a well-designed recipe suitable for a dry red wine. The following recipe, based mainly on elderberries as the red fruit, would be a typical example.

| | | |
|---|---|---|
| Red grape concentrate | 10fl oz | 280ml |
| Elderberries | 3lbs | 1362g |
| Sugar | 1lb 8oz | 681g |

This recipe design, with respect to total acidity (about 0.45%) and final alcohol (about 12%), is perfectly respectable for a dry table wine, although the total tannin level, approaching 0.2%, suggests some harshness in the wine when young. So Joe sets about making his wine. Taking care to sterilise the elderberries, he pasteurises them by taking them just to boiling point in about 1 litre of water, cooling them before crushing, and transferring them to a fermentation bin with the grape concentrate, dissolved sugar and water in a total of about three-litres. At this stage he will add any necessary pectolase and nutrients and, oh yes, the yeast! He finds a sachet of suitable dried yeast, starts it according to the instructions, and 2-4 hours later adds it to the must. He then proceeds with a normal four-day pulp fermentation, then strains into a one-gallon jar, topping up with water, and fermenting to dryness. So what has he done wrong so far? How could he improve? Let us consider how he has tackled his fermentation.

First, the yeast. Although our winemaker has made this his last consideration, I strongly advocate that the yeast should be one of the first and most important issues to be tackled. With the recipe formulated, at least in skeleton form at first, the winemaker should prime the yeast at least 2-4 days before picking the elderberries. As soon as the yeast has been activated, it should be fed it with a little of the diluted red grape concentrate, which will be used in the recipe.

The best way to do this is to dilute the grape concentrate fivefold and use it to double the volume of the yeast starter approximately every four hours until all the grape concentrate has been added. After two days the yeast starter should be growing vigorously in a volume of about 1.5 litres. This is now the optimum time to prepare the elderberries. When the yeast is added to the elderberries and sugar in the fermentation bucket, the primary fermentation, the phase where the yeast multiplies rapidly due to the high energy obtained from the dissolved oxygen in the must, will be over in a matter of hours. Creating a short primary fermentation like this is extremely advantageous, as many contaminating organisms require oxygen to survive, and will have no chance to multiply once a hostile anaerobic environment has been established. Contrast this with our winemaker's fermentation where the yeast will often take days to grow to sufficient numbers before entering the anaerobic fermentation stage. During this time any contaminating organisms have been given ample opportunity to feed on the sugar and nutrients in the must. Even when the winemaker's yeast strain eventually establishes itself and prevents further growth of the contaminating microbes, the damage will already have been done, as unwanted off flavours will already have been produced as a result of metabolism of the sugar and other energy sources. So our winemaker must learn to think ahead, and prime a good yeast strain in advance in order to cut down this lag phase before the yeast shoots into exponential growth.

Some industrial fermentation vessels have capacities as high as 100,000 litres. These are inoculated with 10,000 litres of the actively-growing organism, which in turn had been expanded from 1,000 litres which had been similarly cultured stepwise from a small culture that had been started in the laboratory. Such examples show that it pays to take care that the fermentation gets off to a perfect start by having prepared a large pure culture of the selected yeast strain before the ingredients are processed.

What else can be done to ensure making a better wine? In the fermentation, fresh elderberries were used.

However, there are distinct advantages in freezing the elderberries in one- or two-pound bags immediately after shredding. Once frozen, they can be used at any time, indeed all year round, thus facilitating the timing of ingredient additions when making a wine. Freezing and thawing also kills a high percentage of the contaminating organisms, making pasteurisation more efficient.

By being able to time the addition of the fruit, in this case elderberries, the winemaker does not necessarily have to add them along with the sugar. Consider the possible advantages of fermenting only the grape concentrate and sugar in a total volume of about 3 litres for a week or two. If this were fermented to dryness, the alcohol content would be above 16%. By monitoring the specific gravity (sg), the elderberries can be crushed and added when the sg is 1.000, immediately lowering the alcohol content to about 12%. This ensures that the elderberry tannins and essences are being extracted from the skins at a much higher alcohol level than they would encounter in a normally conducted fermentation. The elderberries give up their tannins and colouring pigments more easily at this higher alcohol concentration. Anyone who doubts this can easily prove the point by soaking a few elderberries in water and comparing this with elderberries soaked in the same volume of 16% alcohol. The colour extraction is far more efficient in the high-alcohol extraction. Thus, adding the elderberries later will lead to faster extraction of tannins, pigments, and flavours during the pulp fermentation, which can now be shortened to one to two days.

Another major advantage of tackling the fermentation in this manner is the improved bouquet in the finished wine, due to the short time the elderberries will have been subjected to losses of their volatile essences by the carbon dioxide produced. How often do you notice the lovely aromas being produced in a room where a wine is being made, and often lasting two to three weeks before fermentation is complete? But when the final clarified wine is inspected, there is a distinct lack of bouquet - hardly surprising as much of the volatiles have slowly been released over the days of fermentation, particularly the pulp fermentation. During the pulp fermentation carried out by our winemaker, the vigorous primary fermentation would have occurred with the elderberries present, with the released carbon dioxide carrying much of the interesting volatile elderberry characteristics into the atmosphere. However, the recommendation of adding the elderberries late preserves most of these volatiles in the must, since the extraction is shorter and the amount of carbon dioxide being released is less, the procedure being closer to marination of the elderberries than pulp fermentation. I have compared many wines made from the same ingredients using the more normal four-day pulp fermentation (with the fruit added early) or the shorter pulp fermentation (with the fruit added late). There can be no doubt that the wines made from the late-added fruit have more bouquet, more character, and are approachable earlier. This is demonstrated in an interesting wine talk 'Are we doing it right?', which is described in the chapter 'Wine Clubs, and Wine Talks'. In this demonstration, each of four different fruit ingredients is added late to the same wine, and it is noted that when a particular fruit is added late the bouquet and flavour of that fruit are accentuated.

This late addition of fruit to add more flavour and character to the final wine is by no means novel, there being many precedents in both the amateur and commercial fields. In Andalucia, sweetening and colouring the sherry with fresh or concentrated grape juice just before shipping produces different sherry styles. Germany frequently holds back some of the original grape juice to sweeten wines just before bottling. Both of these techniques allow the quality of these wines to be improved by these late additions of grape juice that still has all its youthful aromas. One of the most renowned wines of all, champagne, owes some of its attributes to the dosage, which is added at the disgorging stage. Again, this late addition of brandy, grape juice, and sugar assures that their freshness will be trapped in the resealed bottle. In the making of some Chianti wines, the fermenting juice of late-maturing grapes is added to the wine after it is made, adding sparkle and youthfulness to the finished wine. Another very novel method has been recorded by one Australian vineyard which allows some uncrushed grapes to stay in the fermenting must until very near the end of the fermentation. At this stage they are crushed, allowing the release into the wine of young fresh aromas from the preserved grapes. A very short further pulp fermentation is all that is required to complete the process. We can also learn from our friends, the beermakers, who often 'dry hop' their product by adding some hops during the maturation of the beer, or use very concentrated hop oil, which is available for the same purpose.

I am convinced that better amateur wine will be made if more attention is paid to the handling of the fermentation. In general, the advice is to ferment all the less-fruity ingredients with the sugar until the bulk of the fermentation has been competed. At this stage, the main fruit should be added and given a short pulp fermentation to produce a wine with a more attractive bouquet, with richer fruit characteristics, and with other subtle improvements. So, winemakers, think ahead, plan ahead, prime that yeast early - you know it makes sense!

# seven
# RECIPE DESIGN

In 1975, a group of enthusiasts from Chilterns and Mid Thames Federation of Wine Guilds formed Chilterns Masters Wine Group, open to anyone with two first prizes in wine or beer classes in Federation-standard competitions. In order to have some long-term aims, the group started to formulate recipes that would produce wines with the character of various commercial styles. Of the many recipes we have designed over the years, two of these, Sauternes and Chianti styles will be described in more detail. The first recipe that was produced, and one of the best, was designed to imitate Sauternes. Using the Sauternes style as an example, I will describe the approach adopted to formulate and taste recipes, until the final decision on the correct ingredients and amounts required giving the style and balance of the wine concerned. The normal time span from conception to completion of a recipe is two to three years. During this time, of course, as many as four different recipes for wine styles will be at various stages of development. At monthly meetings, evenings tasting these wine-style recipes are interspersed with evenings enjoying other wine topics such as Taste Tests, Unusual Commercial Wines, and Blind Tastings.

For the first Sauternes evening, the group had agreed that each member would make a sweet white wine as near to Sauternes in style as could be managed. At this stage the winemakers had complete freedom to use ingredients of their own choice. Chateau Filhot Sauternes 1976 was chosen as the standard commercial wine showing all the recognised characteristics, with a deep golden colour, superb botrytis bouquet, complex flavour, perfect balance, and the hallmark of all great wines, a long lingering farewell.

How could we, the amateur winemakers, match this? We couldn't. Eight skilled winemakers had all produced good sweet white wines, but nowhere near the Chateau Filhot in quality or style. Our wines were more like sweetened versions of a dry white table wine, lacking the body, alcohol, and depth of flavour of the Sauternes. Disillusioned, we blended a few of the wines, finding that a blend of a rhubarb and strawberry wine and an apple wine was closer to the flavour than any others. As it was suggested that some grape concentrate would improve the blend, our host searched out a sweet heavy wine made from nearly twice the normal amount of white grape concentrate. The suggestion proved to be valuable as the addition of his wine improved the blend, adding more body and getting closer to the flavour, although it was agreed that we were still a long way off. It was decided to make a wine based on the ingredients in the final blend that we had just tasted, and that we would sample the wine in about six-months time.

This was the design of the recipe for one gallon.

| | |
|---|---|
| White grape concentrate (CWE) | 10fl oz |
| Apple juice | 36fl oz |
| White grape juice (Stute) | 4fl oz |
| Rhubarb | 16oz |
| Honey (Ratcliffe, set) | 6oz |
| Strawberries | 5oz |
| Sugar | 26oz |

High alcohol yeast was used, fermenting to dryness and sweetening to a specific gravity of about 1.030. When tasted six months later, the wine was well received, certainly showing some of the desired characteristics. We reckoned that we could beneficially increase the rhubarb and the honey, perhaps increase the strawberries, and try the addition of banana. In order to glean as much information as possible from the next tasting, a table was drawn up (Sauternes Mark 1)) with six different variations of the quantities of fruits used. All the winemakers in the group would make one of these recipes, with the wines to be tasted and evaluated six months later.

**Sauternes Mark 1 (1gallon)**

| | A | B | C | D | E | F |
|---|---|---|---|---|---|---|
| Rhubarb, oz | 32 | 32 | 32 | 32 | 32 | 32 |
| White grape concentrate, fl oz | 14 | 14 | 14 | 14 | 14 | 14 |
| Banana, oz | | 8 | - | - | 8 | 8 |
| Apple juice, fl oz | 40 | 40 | 40 | 40 | 40 | 40 |
| Set honey, oz | 4 | 4 | 4 | 8 | 8 | 8 |
| Glycerol, fl oz | 2 | 2 | 2 | 2 | 2 | 2 |
| Strawberry, oz | 4 | 4 | 8 | 4 | 8 | 4 |
| Sugar, oz | 27 | 26 | 26 | 26 | 25 | 26 |

**Tasting of Sauternes Mark 1**

At the tasting the best wine was D, showing a very attractive bouquet with hints of botrytis and a well-balanced complex flavour. The banana was noticeable in wines made by B, E, and F, and did not push the style in the right direction. The two wines with 8oz strawberries were deep in colour and had replaced the subtle hint of botrytis with a more obvious strawberry character. The wines with only 4oz honey appeared less rich and rounded than the others. Little fault could be found with wine D which stood up well to the commercial, again Chateau Filhot 1976. Our decision was that each of us would repeat recipe D, calling this our amateur standard, and, in addition, we would each do one variation. The variations were; no honey, 12oz honey, 16oz honey, no rhubarb, no strawberry, and 50% more rhubarb and strawberry. So off we went to our demijohns for Sauternes Mark 2.

**Tasting of Sauternes Mark 2**

The Chateau Filhot 1976, costing £6.00 in 1981 (and now around £30.00 for the 1990 vintage), was excellent, showing the typical style that we were trying to imitate. Initially the amateur standards, Mark 1D, were tasted and found to be not only satisfyingly very similar to each other, but also to be surprisingly similar to the commercial. In some the honey might have been a trifle obvious, but these wines were all less than six months old and probably needed more time for the ingredients to marry. When the variations that had been made were tasted, all the wines were good and interesting, but all lacked the excellent balance and Sauternes-type quality of the Mark 1D standard wines that we had tasted earlier that evening. As it appeared that the amounts of the ingredients in our standard recipe had now been optimised, we agreed to each cellar one bottle of the standard and one bottle of the variation that we had made. The plan was then to retaste in one year's time to reassess the wines. This time we just had to wait, turning our attention to other subjects for the next year.

**Second tasting of Sauternes Mark 2, one year later**

Marvellous. Apart from a little spritzig in a couple of wines that had started to referment, the wines were all stable with the odd slight deposit. The verdict was the same as a year ago, with the standards all showing good qualities not far from Chateau Filhot (which we had to taste again to refresh our memories!). The variations all lacked something necessary for Sauternes style. Before we decided to settle on recipe 1D as our final selection for a Sauternes-style recipe, we did some further honing over the next year to produce our final version (Sauternes Mark 3). Full instructions for making this recipe are included under Sweet White Table Wines in the chapter 'A Selection of Recipes'.

**Sauternes Mark 3 (one gallon)**

| | | |
|---|---|---|
| White grape concentrate | 13fl oz | 368ml |
| Apple juice | 35fl oz | 1 litre |
| Glycerol | 2fl oz | 57ml |
| Rhubarb | 32oz | 907g |

**Sauternes Mark 3 (one gallon) continued**

| | | |
|---|---|---|
| Clover honey | 8oz | 227g |
| Strawberries | 4oz | 113g |
| Sugar | 21oz | 595g |

The Sauternes recipe has become extremely popular in the Chilterns and Middlesex area, and its fame has even spread to the wilds of Norfolk. Why so popular? I feel that not only does the recipe produce a very sound sweet white wine showing commercial characteristics, but also that the blend of ingredients results in great consistency from batch to batch. This is often described as having a large window for the amounts and quality of the fruits used, resulting in little variation in the end product. Thus differences in rhubarb or honey from year to year play no major role in influencing the quality of the wine. Similarly, this is one wine, which proves to have very little variation in quality irrespective of who makes the wine. I remember stewarding at Wycombe Show for the judge who was finalising the sweet white class from four wines, which were excellent and very similar. No wonder - they had all been made to the Sauternes recipe by members of Chilterns Masters. I have tried many times to improve the recipe, making some very interesting wines by adding extra ingredients but always failing to make a better Sauternes-style wine. The one thing I always do with this recipe, however, is to add the strawberries very late in the fermentation when the sg has fallen below 1.000. This procedure of 'late fruiting' was fully described in the chapter on Ingredients And How To Use Them.

With our confidence boosted, Chilterns Masters Wine Guild experimented with many other wine styles, but we soon realised that the recipes were not all as easy to formulate as the Sauternes had been. We realised that we had been quite fortunate in our original choice of ingredients for the Sauternes, being fairly close to the final blend of fruits and honey. In order to determine the fruits required to make the different styles of wine, it proved necessary to cover a wider range of ingredients initially. Although this meant that the recipes took longer to produce, our patience was rewarded, and we produced recipes for Claret, Beaujolais, Burgundy, Table Rosé, Table White, and Red and White After-Dinner Wines. These were published about 12 years ago in a small booklet by Chilterns Masters Guild. More recently, Chilterns Masters have finished recipes for Sauvignon Blanc, Chardonnay, and Chianti, and are currently working on Sercial, Gewürztraminer, Tokai, and port. Our Chianti recipe has only recently reached completion, and I will use this as an example of how we now construct our final recipes for specific wine types. Normally, we read tasting notes for the style we are trying to emulate, and choose what would appear to be appropriate fruits to use. However, there was not much easily-found information on Chianti. Jancis Robinson describes Chianti as high acid, farmyardy, with dense pluminess when made from fully ripe grapes. Victor Hazan says look for flowery, spiced bouquet, showing oak, dried fruits, and herbs in the palate. The only answer was to turn up with our own efforts at Chianti and see how they compared with commercial examples.

At our first Chianti tasting, the first of two commercial wines selected was Chianti Rufina 1990 (Tesco, £3.69). This wine had a good youthful colour with a light fruity bouquet. The wine was clean with a good balance showing softening tannins. Our second commercial was a 1990 Chianti Classico (Asda, £3.89). This wine had a more mature colour, and a definite cherry-type bouquet and flavour - a clean, well-balanced wine. Of the amateur wines tasted, the only one showing Chianti-type qualities was a wine made from grape concentrate, elderberry, banana, and Morello cherry. There were suggestions that blackberry might be equally suitable to Morello cherry, and that small amounts of raspberry or strawberry could help to produce Chianti type characteristics. We therefore drew up a table with four different recipes designed to show if blackberry was preferable to Morello cherry or a mixture of the two, or if the addition of raspberry or strawberry made any improvement to the wine. The table below for Chianti Mark 1 shows the ingredients used, all ten members of the group making at least one of the four recipes for tasting within the next year.

## Chianti Mark 1 (1 gallon)

|  | A | B | C | D |
|---|---|---|---|---|
| Red grape concentrate, fl oz | 16 | 16 | 16 | 16 |
| Bottled Morello cherries, oz | 16 | 16 | - | 8 |
| Bottled blackberries, oz | - | - | 16 | 8 |
| Raspberries, oz | 2 | - | 2 | 1 |
| Strawberries, oz | - | 2 | - | 1 |
| Sugar, oz | 19 | 19 | 19 | 19 |

## Tasting of Chianti Mark 1
After tasting the same two commercial wines, Chianti Rufina and Chianti Classico, the wines made by group A using bottled Morello cherries and a small addition of raspberry were found to be closest to the commercials. These wines, however, lacked depth of colour, which could possibly be achieved by including elderberry in the recipe. Three groups then made the recipes for Chianti Mark 2, designed to show if elderberry was a suitable additional ingredient.

## Chianti Mark 2 (1 gallon)

|  | A | B | C |
|---|---|---|---|
| Red grape concentrate, fl oz | 20 | 20 | 20 |
| Bottled Morello cherries, oz | 16 | 16 | 16 |
| Elderberries, oz | 4 | 10 | 16 |
| Raspberries, oz | 2 | 2 | 2 |
| Sugar, oz | 16 | 16 | 16 |

## Tasting of Chianti Mark 2, 7 months later
There was no doubt that the best wines were the ones made with 10oz and 16oz elderberries per gallon. Although one or two of these were still on the young side, they showed good Chianti characteristics, more like the Classico than the Rufina. Our decision was to make Chianti Mark 3 using this recipe with 16oz elderberries, and allowing each winemaker to add one twist. For example, the recipe could be left as it is, or more fruit could be added, or the wine could be oaked. The winemakers were also asked to note the brand of red grape concentrate that they used for their wines. The recipes for Chianti Mark 3 and Chianti Mark 4 are shown later in the text.

## Tasting of Chianti Mark 3, 12 months later
The consensus was that the wines were true-to-style, but were a little high in alcohol when compared to the commercials. It was also felt that the 16oz elderberry was a little on the high side. The wines made with Solvino Italian Classic red grape concentrate were more Chianti-like. Some subtle variations were obtained with the additions of about 2oz strawberries or blackcurrants. Feeling that we were now very close to imitating Chianti style, we agreed to make Chianti Mark 4 using the Solvino concentrate and a reduced elderberry content of 12oz. Again the wines could be tweaked slightly to add slight variations to the wines.

|  | Chianti Mark 3 | Chianti Mark 4 |
|---|---|---|
| Red grape concentrate, fl oz | 20 | 20 (Solvino) |
| Bottled Morello cherries, oz | 16 | 16 |
| Elderberries, oz | 16 | 12 |
| Raspberries, oz | 2 | 2 |
| Sugar, oz | 16 | 16 |

## Tasting of Chianti Mark 4, 12 months later

Six wines were compared against the commercial, 1996 Chianti Coli Senesi (Oddbins, £4.49) Typical comments on this 12% alcohol wine were that it had hints of cherry and strawberry, and was very firm in the palate with a long enjoyable aftertaste. All our six wines compared most favourably with the commercial. As cherry was part of the basic recipe, all our wines showed this flavour to some degree. Variations such as small additions of blackcurrant, redcurrant, blackberry, or strawberry added subtle differences to the wines. We decided that our final Chianti recipe would be as for Mark 4 above, but that slight variations could be produced by other small additions. My personal prefence is for the recipe below. The ingredients would, of course, be treated as in the chapter on 'Ingredients And How To Use Them', by processing the red grape concentrate and sugar first in a volume of about 3 litres. After at least a week, the rest of the fruit and oak would be added for a 2 day pulp fermentation.

## The Final Chianti (1 gallon)

| | | |
|---|---|---|
| Red grape concentrate (Solvino) | 20fl oz | 568ml |
| Bottled Morello cherries | 16 oz | 454g |
| Elderberries | 12 oz | 340g |
| Raspberries | 2oz | 58g |
| Strawberries | 4oz | 113g |
| Sugar | 16oz | 454g |
| Oak shavings | 1oz | 28g |

Further maturation with oak strips, as discussed in the chapter Oak, has added smoothness and maturity to this Chianti which has been tasted and appreciated by a wide range of National Judges, and has already had a first award at a major show. The development of these two recipes for Sauternes and Chianti could certainly be done by one person alone, but is so much more easily done in groups of 6-10 people. Working in groups has the added satisfaction of a good social evening with other enthusiasts. I can only encourage this approach, even if it is solely used to improve existing recipes.

# eight
# A VERSATILE WINE

This chapter describes how one wine can be blended to make five different styles of wine.

Although I had been aware of the potential of blending wines for many years, I had never considered this beyond mixing various percentages of similar-style wines in order to produce a wine more balanced than any of the unblended wines. Commercially, this is fairly standard practice with a cellarman blending different grape varieties to produce a product varying little from year to year. Blending different grape varieties produces many of the classic wines in the commercial world. Claret is a fine example, with high percentages of Cabernet Sauvignon and Merlot being softened with as little as 5-10% Cabernet Franc.

For the amateur, blending is one of the easiest ways of reducing the acidity in high-acid wines, or of lowering the tannin in red wines produced from high levels of very tannic fruits such as elderberry. As with the example of claret above, often the addition of as little as 5-10% of one wine can significantly improve the quality of the final blend, giving desirable characteristics such as a floral bouquet or an improvement in the farewell of the wine. In the last few days before a wine show, countless amateurs are blending, tasting, and occasionally spitting, as they blend their wines to produce the near-perfect flavour and balance.

I had started to organise myself a few days before a show when I realised that the batch of wine I had intended to use for my dry and medium white wines was badly oxidised, and I could find no other suitable batch. I had also agreed to produce the dry white wine for our club entry in the three-bottle class. So there I was with a show next weekend and no white table wines. Well, that's not exactly true as I had a large batch of a base wine for Sauternes style (see chapter on 'Recipe Design') that I had made recently. Examination of that rhubarb, apple, and strawberry recipe shows that it was designed to finish dry at 14-15% alcohol, subsequent sweetening reducing the alcohol content to nearer 13-14%. I had made the wine exactly as the recipe indicated with enough additional sugar to produce 15-16% when bone dry. My reasoning behind this was that, with a dry wine at 15-16% alcohol, I had more choices in the method of sweetening the base wine to produce a sweet white table wine. Ignoring acidity for the moment, as this can always be adjusted later, there is a variety of ways that the dry wine can be sweetened in order to construct a wine with the necessary balance. The base wine, if fermented out completely, should have a specific gravity (sg) of about 0.990. The degree of sweetness required in sweet white wines of this style is usually found around sg 1.030, although this will vary for different batches of wine. If a litre of the wine is sweetened with granulated sugar until sg 1.030 is reached, the volume will increase by 65ml, concomitantly decreasing the alcohol by about 0.9%. For my base wine above, at 15-16%, this would reduce the alcohol to between 14 and 15%. Only tasting the wine will tell its quality and balance. Most good Sauternes are at least this degree of sweetness with an alcohol content of about 14%. Before rounding off the balance of this wine with sugar, and/or acid, and/or base wine, let us examine some of the other possibilities that exist for sweetening the base wine.

White grape concentrate will add sweetness, acidity, and body to the wine. About 100ml grape concentrate (although this will vary depending on the brand used) will be required to raise 1 litre of base wine to sg 1.030, reducing the alcohol concentration by about 1.4%. A judicious mixture of these two sweeteners, sugar and grape concentrate, could well be the answer to honing the end product to produce a well-balanced sweet white wine. Another method of sweetening is to add white grape juice which has a similar acidity to the base wine. With an initial sg of 1.070, however, it would require equal amounts of white grape juice and base wine in order to produce a wine with sg 1.030. This would lower the alcohol to about 8%, too low for this style of wine. In practice I find that the best method of sweetening is to add sugar to sg 1.015, then mix grape concentrate to 1.030, then round off the balance with additions of white grape juice or base wine, with a final touch of acidity if necessary. The great advantage of finding the perfect balance by fine tuning with white grape juice is that it is so easily done, small additions not having such a dramatic effect on sweetness as additions of sugar or white grape concentrate. From my base wine I duly made the sweet white wine that I needed for the show. The sweetened wine was left in a litre bottle, since blends such as this invariably throw minor precipitates, which take time to settle.

A second style of wine I needed for the show was a fruit white sweet. For this class, quite a range of alcohol levels and weight of wine would be acceptable, although the heavier wines are usually more favoured. My first blend was very close, being achieved by adding sugar to the base wine until sg 1.010 was reached, and by rounding off the wine with white grape concentrate until a suitable degree of sweetness/acidity was obtained. At sg 1.034 I found I had a very promising sweet white fruit wine with a powerful bouquet and flavour. Although this wine had similarities with the sweet white table wine above, it showed more flavour, sweetness, body, alcohol, and acidity. Right then, no problem with the sweet white wines, but what of the drier styles?

I then wondered if I could do anything else with this base wine; a dry wine with 15% alcohol, lots of body, and strong flavour. I needed a dry white table wine with an alcohol content of about 12%. When I mixed 4 parts of the base wine with 1 part of water, I was amazed at the result. I had produced a wine not only with 12% alcohol but also with an attractive bouquet and flavour, eminently suitable for a dry white wine style. The acidity was a little low but easily adjusted. The lowering of the fruit content with water had given the correct depth of flavour for this wine style. Again, this dry white could be pitched to its perfect balance with base wine, water, or acid.

I now needed a medium white table wine, normally about 10-11% alcohol and sg about 1.010. I took 11 parts of base wine and 4 parts of white grape juice, giving me a wine around 11% alcohol and sg 1.011. The wine, however, was not balanced for the class with rather strong harsh flavours being accentuated with high acidity. In order to reduce the acidity I made another effort by mixing 11 parts base wine and 4 parts of a sugar solution at sg 1.070. This was better, but was now a touch bland. However, mixing equal volumes of the two wines I had just sweetened, I found that I was in the right ball park with a wine showing good flavour, and a pleasant balance of acidity, sugar, and alcohol. The wine improved with a smidgen of white grape juice. Alternatively, if the wine had required more flavour, I could have used more base wine. If necessary, similar adjustments could be made with acid, sugar solution, or water. Again, as with the sweet wines, this type of blend is prone to precipitations or hazes and is best left in a cool area for a few days for any particulate matter to settle. If this is done in a litre bottle, the clear wine can be racked off for the show bottle, leaving a glass or two of wine for the winemaker.

I then turned my attention to the rosé medium wine, wondering if I could possibly adapt my base wine for the rosé class. In the Sparkling Wine chapter in this book I show how a medium-sweet sparkling wine can be made by the addition of 34ml sweetened raspberry juice to about 700ml wine just after the disgorging of the wine. I thought that I would try a similar addition of raspberry juice, aiming for 12% alcohol and sg 1.010. This would require first diluting the base wine exactly as had been done to make the dry white table wine, and then adding the freshly prepared raspberry juice. The sweetened raspberry juice was made by dissolving sugar in clear raspberry juice until no more sugar would dissolve, as described in the Medium Sweet Sparkling Wine recipe in the chapter 'A Selection of Recipes'. The ratio of 34ml sweetened raspberry juice to 700ml base wine would be fine for the required rosé colour and flavour, but the finished wine would be too sweet. The solution was to make some unsweetened raspberry juice, and use 30ml of this and 30ml sweetened juice to 1 litre of the dry white table wine. The total amounts of water, raspberry juices, and base wine needed to produce the rosé are summarised below. The rosé needed to be a little sweeter, this being achieved by careful addition of sweetened raspberry juice, tasting until a balance suitable for medium rosé was attained. If a more intense hue in the colour was required, a little red wine could be added until an acceptable depth of colour was produced.

I had now produced five different wine styles by various blends of the dry white base wine of about 15% alcohol. A summary of how to construct these five wines follows.

**Base wine**

Below is the recipe that was developed in the chapter 'Recipe Design'.

**Recipe for Sauternes-style wine**

| | | |
|---|---|---|
| White grape concentrate | 13fl oz | 368ml |
| Apple juice | 35fl oz | 1 litre |
| Glycerol | 2fl oz | 57ml |
| Rhubarb | 32oz | 907g |
| Clover honey | 8oz | 227g |
| Strawberries | 4oz | 113g |
| Sugar | 21oz | 595g |

**Sweet white table wine**

To 1 litre of base wine add granulated sugar to reach sg 1.015. Add white grape concentrate to reach sg 1.030, and round off the balance with white grape juice or base wine.

**Sweet white fruit wine**

To 1 litre of base wine add granulated sugar to reach sg 1.010, then add white grape concentrate until a suitable degree of sweetness is obtained, usually about sg 1.034.

**Dry white table wine**

Take 800ml base wine plus 200ml water, adjusting the balance with acid, water, and base wine as required.

**Medium white table wine**

To 1.1 litres base wine add 200ml white grape juice and 200ml sugar solution at sg 1.070. Any necessary adjustment should be done with acid and any of the three ingredients used.

**Medium rosé wine**

To 800ml base wine add 200ml water, 30ml sweetened raspberry juice, and 30ml unsweetened raspberry juice, again fine tuning for the perfect balance with the same ingredients.

All these wines were then left in litre bottles in a cool place in order to allow any precipitates to settle. A week later all five wines were racked into show bottles and entered in Chilterns and Mid Thames Festival Show. The results were outstanding. As the table white sweet wine had always done well and was the style that the base wine had been designed to produce, it was no surprise to find that it had been awarded first place. Most pleasing, however, was to find that the medium white table wine and the medium rosé table wine were also top of their classes. The fruit sweet white was third, the comment card indicating "a good wine with highish alcohol and a hot finish". On retasting the wine I could only agree with the comment. The dry white table wine, also third, was described by the judge as a very promising wine with strong flavours that needed time to marry and mellow. As the base wine was less than two months old, and the heavy flavours had been chosen to suit a sweet wine style, the judge's comments again made good sense. So one wine had been used to make five different wine styles, all of which stood up well in their respective classes.

There can be no doubt that the winemaker can design a base wine, which can be blended to make different style wines. Advantages of making wines this way is that only one large batch of wine has to be made. As this wine is 15-16% alcohol, there are seldom any of the oxidation or contamination problems invariably associated with lighter-style lower-alcohol wines. The different styles can be blended on the spot as I have proved when giving talks at wine circles. It is a most impressive demonstration for the audience. Much of this work is still experimental, and I am trying the same with a red wine base. Another advantage of this approach is that once a blend has been identified as successful, the contents of the wine can be estimated and scaled up to make a gallon of a particular wine type. As far as the five wines listed above are concerned, I still often use these blends, having absorbed the notes from the judges on the comment cards, e.g., reducing the alcohol of the sweet white fruit wine, and diluting the dry white to nearer 11% alcohol improved the quality of both blends. Give it a try - you'll be amazed how easy it is.

# nine
# SPARKLING WINES

You go to my head like the bubbles in a glass of fine Burgundy brew (adapted from the song *You Go to My Head* by Coots and Gillespie).

For me, no book on wine would be complete without a chapter on sparkling wines, because I consider that this style of wine is as much a work of art as it is a labour of love. The lyrics above are so true, as sparkling wines give the effect of intoxication far more quickly than drinking the same strength still wine. When sparkling wine is taken into the palate, the carbon dioxide released volatilises some of the alcohol, which is inhaled directly to the lungs where it is quickly absorbed into the bloodstream, reaching the brain in seconds. The second effect arrives soon after when the normal absorption of alcohol from the digestive system in turn reaches the brain, resulting in a very pleasurable additive sensation. Of course, the canny Scots knew this years ago as can be seen in any bar in the north of Scotland where every counter has a bottle of free lemonade. The smart local dilutes his dram of whisky with an equal volume of lemonade and gets greater alcohol mileage for his money!

I became interested in making sparkling wine when I read 'Making Wines Like Those you Buy' by Bryan Acton and Peter Duncan and 'How to Make Wines With a Sparkle' by John Restle and Don Hebbs. However, I was somewhat disillusioned as Méthode Champenoise appeared to be too tortuous and time consuming. As the Sparklett would obviously produce an inferior product and the equipment was not available for other methods of carbon dioxide impregnation, I wondered what else was possible. Could there be a faster, simpler method? Carbon dioxide at room temperature is, of course, a gas and there is about 4.5 litres of carbon dioxide dissolved in a 750ml bottle of champagne. This is equivalent to six atmospheres, although four atmospheres is recommended as sufficient for amateur winemaking. At temperatures below -80°C, carbon dioxide is a solid, and 6.5g of this solid would be required to give the three litres of gas required for four atmospheres of pressure in a normal bottle size. I found a source of solid carbon dioxide (dry ice), and returned home with some in a suitable unsealed thermos flask.

In an attempt to make instant sparkling wine, I prepared myself with a once used champagne bottle filled with still wine to 2in from the top, a hollow plastic cork, a piece of nylon, some very thin wire, a wire cage, and a pair of pliers. As I had a slight apprehension that this might not be the safest of manipulations, I also had acquired a white boiler suit, a chemist's mask with a plastic visor covering my whole face, and a pair of shoulder length asbestos gloves. I decided that this experiment was best carried out in the back end of my garage. I put a piece of carbon dioxide weighing 6.5g, about the size of a pea, in the hollow plastic cork, tied it quickly with the piece of very thin wire, hammered the cork into the champagne bottle, immediately tied on the wire cage, inverted the bottle in a bucket of ice/water, and ran.

I had just cleared the garage door when there was an almighty bang. I gingerly returned into the garage to find that there was not a piece of glass of any notable size. The cork was also ripped apart. The sequel to this story comes from my neighbour who was mowing his lawn when he heard the bang. He told me later that, looking at me in my boiler suit, facemask, and gloves, he thought the Martians had landed! I humbly decided that, maybe for once, the French were right, and that the only sensible way to make sparkling wine was by Méthode Champenoise.

So what is Méthode Champenoise? What is the winemaker trying to achieve in the making of sparkling wine? Before answering this, it is necessary to analyse what the winemaker is doing in the making of a normal dry white wine of about 12% alcohol by volume. The equation below shows the fermentation of sugar to alcohol and carbon dioxide, a process carried out by a cascade of enzymes, which are secreted by the yeast cells.

$$C_{12}H_{22}O_{11} \quad = \quad 4C_2H_5OH \quad + \quad 4CO_2$$

| $C_{12}H_{22}O_{11}$ | $4C_2H_5OH$ | $4CO_2$ |
|---|---|---|
| Sucrose | Ethyl alcohol | Carbon dioxide |
| 342g | 184g | 176g (89.6 litres) |

For observant readers who note that the figures on either side of the equation do not add up, the reason is that sucrose is first hydrolysed to glucose and fructose gaining one molecule of water ($H_2O$, 18g) in the process. Much carbon dioxide is released during the fermentation, amounting to well over 200 litres from a normal one-gallon jar, which would have started with about 900g sugar. So beware of pets sleeping on the floor in a room with poor ventilation and many large-scale fermentations! It is this production of carbon dioxide, which is all-important in creating the bubbles in sparkling wine. Assume that a stable, clarified dry white wine has been made under normal conditions with an alcohol content of 10%. This still wine now needs to be converted into sparkling wine by the addition of sugar and yeast, and by allowing the secondary fermentation to take place in a Champagne-style bottle. Commercially, the best sparkling wines have about 6 atmospheres of carbon dioxide, i.e., about 4.5 litres per standard 75cl bottle. To achieve this, the addition of 17g sugar per bottle would be required.

However, the amateur must tone down these additions for the following reasons. This high pressure is required to produce the best styles of sparkling wine, especially in Champagne. Commercially, they accept that a percentage of their bottles will break during the secondary fermentation. Although this is a hazard, which the commercial world is willing to accept in order to produce these pressures, this is a hazard which the amateur winemaker wishes to avoid. In addition, commercially, the bottles are new each time a sparkling wine is made, while the amateur is faced with using bottles that have been used at least once. It is, therefore, best to consider that 4 atmospheres, equivalent to 11-12g sugar per bottle, is the maximum pressure that the amateur need attempt to produce. Unfortunately, we cannot just add the calculated amount of sugar, prime with yeast, and allow it to ferment, because there may still be some fermentable sugar in the still wine. If this were to ferment along with the added sugar, dangerous levels of carbon dioxide could be produced. It is for this reason that the amount of residual sugar needs to be determined. The two simplest methods for the amateur are by specific gravity (sg) and by testing for residual reducing sugars, in this case glucose and fructose. Looking first at the specific gravity method, most commercial white wines finish very close to sg 0.990. In order to produce 4 atmospheres of carbon dioxide, 11.5g sugar would need to be added to every 75cl bottle. This amount would raise the sg of such a wine to 0.996. Few amateur wines ferment out to such a low sg, most finishing around sg 0.995 due mainly to unfermentable sugars in the ingredients used. This is why, in making my own sparkling wines, I am willing to go as high as sg 1.002 provided I do not use more than 11.5g sugar per bottle or 69g sugar per 4.5 litres, although this last figure should be nearer 74g for a full gallon jar which contains almost 5 litres (see chapter 'Equipment'). However, competitors entering the National Guild of Wine and Beer Competition should note that they are restricted to adding just over 9g sugar per bottle, equivalent to 56g per 4.5 litres. Wines that have specific gravities over 0.995 should not be used for making sparkling wines, as we do not know the type of residual sugars. Occasionally, residual fructose and glucose may not have fermented completely, and this could lead to undesirable high pressures in the bottles. On the other hand, we could have unfermentable oligosaccharides which could slowly break down to give fermentable sugars which would add to the pressures produced in the secondary fermentation of the added sugar.

The Clinitest for reducing sugars, which will not detect recently-added sucrose (granulated sugar), should give a reading of less than 0.25% in a wine that has completed fermentation and is stable. I think it is still worth finding the specific gravity, as it is so easily done and can show the presence of non-reducing oligosaccharides, which could pose problems in the secondary fermentation. Therefore, wines above 0.25% in the Clinitest or above specific gravities of 0.995 should not be used for sparkling wines.

One other aspect of the still wine that we have to consider is its suitability to make a quality sparkling wine. Firstly, the wine will have been racked and clarified to produce a star bright wine. If the wine is not crystal clear when the secondary fermentation is started, it cannot be expected to be so when the yeast is removed some months later. The style of the wine is important, with the lighter fresher styles usually making the better sparkling wines. Alcohol should be about 10% with a wide range of acceptable acidity depending on the particular wine style. One point to note is that, in the process of producing four atmospheres of pressure, the alcohol content will be raised by about 1%. This increased alcohol level, plus the carbon dioxide produced, will have quite an effect on the balance of the wine. What was a perfect balance in the still wine may not be so in the sparkling version. Therefore, it pays to have well-tried and trusted recipes that will produce the required product. In my opinion, the acidic carbon dioxide is detected more on the centre of the tongue than the other fruit acids (accepted as being detected on the sides of the tongue), and, surprisingly, causes the sparkling wine to taste less acidic than it would as a still wine due to the two sensations occurring at once in different areas of the taste buds. Perhaps this is why the high-acidic musts used to make champagne are so successful.

Another requirement of the basic wine is that treatment with metabisulphite should be kept to a minimum. Once the wine has started its bottle fermentation, there is no danger of oxidation as the bottle is sealed and the wine is saturated with four atmospheres of carbon dioxide. Equally, if the wine has recently been treated with metabisulphite before the bottle fermentation, there will be no chance for the sulphur dioxide to be neutralised, and, when the bottle is opened, sulphur dioxide will be noticeable. Therefore, there is no need for metabisulphite treatment during the final racking and clarification, provided the bottle fermentation is started as soon as possible. The ingredients used for the primary fermentation should be sterilised with metabisulphite as usual.

And so to the secondary fermentation. A good champagne yeast should be used, e.g., Gervin no. 6, strain 8906. This yeast ferments very efficiently for both still wines and sparkling wines, and its sediment is easily removed, an important requirement in making this style of wine. I remember being in Schramsberg in Napa Valley watching two men vibrating bottles on a machine to try and disturb a 'rogue yeast' that was clinging to the glass. They were clad in leather boiler suits and gloves, and had protective face visors for this hazardous task. They had a batch of thousands of bottles that were affected, highlighting the importance of a good settling yeast for making sparkling wines.

By far the most efficient way to start the secondary fermentation is to prime the yeast with a little water, then add an equal volume of white grape juice an hour later. Add the appropriate amount of sugar to the still wine in a gallon jar, and use this to keep doubling the volume of the yeast starter every hour. When at a volume of about 1 litre, leave until the release of carbon dioxide shows that the fermentation is well under way, and then add to the gallon jar. The wine may now be bottled in champagne bottles, the best ones all weighing over 2lbs when empty. Although I have recycled such bottles many times with no problems, they should be inspected before use for chips and scratches, any doubtful bottles being immediately discarded. The bottles will, of course, have been cleaned and treated with a sterilising solution. They should be filled to 2 inches below the top of the bottle, and closed with a hollow plastic cork, which is tied down with a wire cage. Commercially, they are closed using crown caps at this stage. Some amateurs also use this method, but the equipment is not readily available, and I find no difficulty in working with the plastic corks. The bottles are now laid horizontally at room temperature, hopefully about 20°C, until a firm deposit appears, usually about 4-6 days. At this stage, they can then be removed to an area where the temperature is about 12-15°C, encouraging a longer, slower fermentation. If such an area does not exist, the bottles can be left at room temperature. Ideally, the wines should rest on their lees for 1-2 years, but they are approachable much earlier. However, the long wait is justified in quality as the wines develop classical champagne style from a long slow autolysis of the yeast cells.

When the wines have been well rested for whatever period of time, the remuage stage is then started. This process, now often called riddling, is used to tease the yeast down to the stopper of the bottle to allow subsequent removal of the yeast. Commercially, this is achieved by placing the bottles in a pupitre which is a wine rack designed to hold the bottles with their tops facing downwards in a series of holes. The wines start off facing slightly downwards from horizontal, and periodically the angle is increased. At the time of increasing the angle, each bottle is given a sharp twist and replaced about an eighth of a turn from its previous position. This helps the yeast to aggregate and slowly sediment leaving the wine above clear. The amateur can easily simulate this by placing the wines in a wine case, and, starting from the horizontal position, slowly raising one end by placing books or similar objects underneath. This process is continued until the bottles are completely upside down, or sur point as they say in France. At this stage, with all the yeast now in the hollow plastic cork, the bottles can be left undisturbed to benefit from further maturation.

The next step is to remove the yeast by the process of disgorging. This can be done by freezing the neck of the bottle in a freezing mixture, removing the cork, topping up if necessary, and recorking the bottle. However, I find the simplest way is to place the inverted bottle into a chest freezer for about an hour until the neck just begins to show signs of freezing. With the bottle still inverted, it is fairly easy to remove the wire cage and push out the stopper, immediately turning the bottle upright. The wine now needs to be topped up with the dosage, which will depend on the style required. If the wine is to be dry, it pays to have some of the original still wine for this manipulation as wines that are incompatible often throw a deposit when blended. Few sparkling wines are bone dry, and adding 30ml white grape juice at this stage softens the wine in the palate, while still leaving the wine dry enough to be acceptable in a dry wine class. The amount of sugar added from 30ml white grape juice is only enough to move the sparkling wine to the dividing line between Extra Brut and Brut, both classified as dry styles. Both the wine and any other addition used for the dosage should be pre-cooled in a refrigerator so that they are compatible with the pre-cooled wine in the bottle. This means that, when poured in carefully, there will be minimal disturbance of the dissolved carbon dioxide in the bottle. If the wine is to be sweet, then the necessary mixture can be added, but this should be done only shortly before drinking or entering a show. This is to avoid a possible re-fermentation, as it is difficult for the amateur to ensure that all the yeast has been removed. The wine, now 1.75-2.0 inches (4.5-5cm) below the top of the bottle, is then recorked and rewired. The wine benefits greatly from a little rest after its traumas. Indeed the wine benefits immensely from a long rest at this stage, especially if 30ml white grape juice has been added. This is due to Reaction Maillard in which sugar and amino acids in the wine react to form compounds responsible for the typical toasted aromas in well-aged sparkling wines.

The dosage stage is quite interesting as it allows the winemaker to change the style of each bottle by varying the contents of the dosage. As above, a dry and a sweet version could be made. The addition of red wine or a whole range of alternatives such as white or red grape concentrate could produce almost any style available commercially. All these styles would have stemmed from the same batch of base wine. Sweetening a dry white sparkling wine with very sweet raspberry juice as described in the Medium Sweet Sparkling Wine in the chapter 'A Selection of Recipes' makes one of my favourite wines. This produces a very refreshing medium-sweet rosé style, which has pleased many judges. Commercially, the dosage is added very similarly, only brandy is also used along with sweetened wine depending on the degree of sweetness required. The increased alcohol content from the brandy helps to inhibit re-fermentation by any residual yeast cells, while also imparting a pleasant flavour, which marries nicely into the wine. Unfortunately, this is not allowed for amateur shows, unless the Sparkling Wine class is in the fortified section.

One suitable alternative to disgorging by ejecting the hollow plastic cork is to use a product called Condessa which has a valve built into a hollow plastic cork. The wine, primed with yeast and sugar, is bottled and stored upright for the fermentation in the bottle. Safety at this stage is guaranteed, as the valve is triggered to open at 5 atmospheres of pressure and release any excess carbon dioxide. After remuage is carried out as previously described, the yeast is removed by pulling a cord to open the valve and discharge the sediment. The stopper can then be removed and the wine topped up as before. The product works well, but the corks are about 80p each and have limited re-usage before they deform.

Although the complete process of making sparkling wine may appear to be long and tortuous, once the conveyor belt is set up the whole process runs very smoothly. One batch can be fermenting to make the still wine, some bottles will be conducting the secondary fermentation, others will be at various angles during the settling of the yeast, while some will be sur point, awaiting the yeast removal. In the commercial world, efforts have been made to lower the man-hours involved in the large-scale production of sparkling wines. During the remuage stage, computerised palettes are used to gently shake the bottles and encourage the yeast to settle more quickly. In many wineries, this has replaced the labour-intensive step of remuage by hand. Another recent development is the encapsulation of the yeast cells in porous sodium alginate beads, allowing the fermentation to occur while the yeast cells are retained in the beads. There is diffusion across the beads of the sugar, the alcohol, and the enzymes secreted by the growing encapsulated yeast cells. When the fermentation is complete, it takes only a few seconds to settle the beads on the cork. I have used this method successfully, but on a small scale it hardly warrants the effort, apart from the pleasure of mastering the technique.

Another very interesting experiment being investigated in the commercial world is the use of a hollow fibre cartridge attached to a crown cap stopper. The device sits in the neck of the bottle and conducts the fermentation using the same diffusion principles as the beads. These very thin hollow fibres are wound up as in a bobbin, and have a very large surface area, allowing extremely efficient diffusion through the fibres. I have tasted wine made in this fashion, and its quality was as good as Méthode Champenoise. One distinct advantage of the hollow fibre cartridge was that the company using these had virtually eliminated breakage that occurs during the secondary fermentation and remuage. Unfortunately, I understand that the costs involved do not yet warrant the introduction of the technique, although I am sure that research is continuing in this area.

ten
OAK

The increased use of oak in amateur winemaking is surely the biggest stride forward since the works of Acton and Duncan and those of Gerry Fowles. Oak maturation has always been a recognised landmark of the commercial wine industry, where we read of quality clarets and red burgundies being matured in new French oak casks. In fact, most quality red wines have had spells in oak from six months to two years. In more recent years, commercial winemakers have been experimenting with oak chips i.e., adding fine pieces of oak to wine maturing in stainless steel tanks, and thus overcoming many of the problems associated with cleaning and sterilising oak barrels.

What then is the best use of oak for the amateur? Many winemakers have fallen heir to used casks, not always oak as walnut and other woods are sometimes used. However, as most high-quality wines are matured only in new oak casks, I question if the old casks are imparting much in the way of oaky character to the wine. An argument people have for the use of old casks is that they aid maturation of the wine due to oxygen exchange across the wood. However, although there is a little 'breathing' of the wine through the wood, most of the oxygen used in maturation comes either from exposure to air during racking, or from air in the ullage space replacing wine evaporated from the barrel. One problem that occurs with casks is that cleaning and sterilisation of these is not a trivial task. The best use of old casks by the amateur is to hold large batches of heavy dessert wines, which are less prone to oxidation and contamination problems. Some winemakers use this as a solera-type maturation system, storing the wine in a 5-gallon cask, and removing one gallon before topping up with a newer similar-style wine.

If oak casks are not the complete answer for the amateur, what are the alternatives? My first experience with oak was about fifteen years ago when I tasted red and dessert wines made by a friend. On two separate occasions, when judging at local wine shows, I realised that I could recognise his dry red and dessert wines. It was as if his fingerprints, or should I say 'palate prints', were all over the wines which all had an elegant oaky/vanilla bouquet and flavour. When asked, he said that he oaked the wines by soaking a few pieces of oak in a litre of wine. These pieces of oak were 0.8 x 1 x 5.5cm. Of course, he worked for one of High Wycombe's many furniture companies. The quality of his wines immediately made me a convert to the use of oak, at least in dry red and dessert styles, or after-dinner wines as they are now called.

Looking around for suitable alternative methods of oaking wines, I used some long slivers of American oak, which were window frame rejects. These were 24mm wide and 6mm thick. As I always made my dry red wines in large batches, I cut the oak down to 48cm lengths that would sit in a 20-litre bottle just like a dipstick. Trial and error was to show me that four strips of the American oak per 20 litres were suitable for oaking my red wines. Immediately before use, the strips were soaked in 10% metabisulphite for 2 minutes, and given a quick rinse. The first time I oaked wines like this, I was impatient, tasting at 1 month and 2 months. By this time there was little indication of oakiness in the wines, although I did learn that the dipsticks made very suitable paddles for stirring the wine. Continuing to taste the wines monthly, there was a noticeable change at 3 to 4 months, with the wines beginning to show oakiness and complexity. From 3 to 6 months, there was a steady increase in these characteristics, while the wines became much smoother beyond 6 months. Ideally, the wine should be oaked for 1 to 2 years. At this time, if the oak is dominating the fruit, the wine can be blended with a similar unoaked wine. I have also recently made some very successful red wines using strips of English oak, and even some kilned English oak. It is interesting to note that the ratio of the surface area of four of these strips to the volume of wine, 1,152 sq cm per 20 litres, is 60% of that of a 225-litre French oak cask which is about 21,500 sq cm per 225 litres. With the speeded diffusion obtained by stirring the wine with the oak strips, the oak maturation of the wine matured in the 20-litre glass vessel could be very similar to that obtained in a 225-litre oak cask.

Now a total convert to the use of oak, I looked at other possibilities to enhance this aspect of my winemaking. In Winemaking in Style, Gerry Fowles recommends the use of American oak granules in both red and white wines, either by using at the start of the fermentation or later if desired. These granules, like very fine sawdust, have a very large surface area, imparting oakiness to the wine in a matter of days. I have found these granules to be excellent at giving oakiness to a finished wine, especially white wines where the short contact time benefits these more delicate styles. The granules need no treatment before use.

Another winemaking friend now appeared on the scene with a large sack of excess American oak from the machining of furniture, from now on referred to as oak shavings. What would we do without High Wycombe's famous furniture industry? I pasteurised the oak by adding water, heating it to over 80°C for 10 minutes, and cooling quickly. I found that adding the cooled shavings and water to the red fruits (1 ounce of oak to the gallon) during a pulp fermentation greatly improved the quality of the red wines. The wines were very approachable at the first racking, appearing much smoother and showing distinct oakiness. These thin shavings have a large surface area, and appear to adsorb some of the harsh tannins from the red fruits in addition to imparting oakiness to the wines. This friend followed up with supplies of English oak, which benefits from a quick blanch and rinse with hot water before pasteurisation as above. Later, I obtained a large sack full of small chips of English oak, very similar in size to the pieces that had been used by the first winemaker I mentioned. The best use I have found for these is addition to a wine after it is racked and clarified. The chips work well both in white and red wines, requiring over 3 months for the red and after-dinner styles, although 1 month is usually sufficient for white wines. Before use, the oak chips are sterilised by soaking in 10% metabisulphite for 2 minutes, then given a quick rinse before being added to the wine at a ratio of 2 chips per litre.

In general, these four oaking techniques may be used in the following ways. For oaking dry red and after-dinner wines, I have settled on a combination of at least two of these options. The best results are obtained by adding oak shavings at 1 ounce to the gallon during the pulp fermentation. There appears to be an excellent relationship between the oak and the red fruits, with the oak imparting flavours into the wine, while adsorbing some of the harsh tannins to such an extent that the wine proves to be smooth and drinkable immediately after racking and settling. Although these wines would undoubtedly improve with time, at this stage I usually further oak mature them in a 20-litre bottle by the addition of the long oak strips, using 4 of these to 20 litres. The maturation of these wines is speeded up by the introduction of air, achieved by siphoning about 2-4 litres of wine into a jug and pouring it back into the 20-litre bottle, stirring with the oak dipsticks. This is done monthly, and also provides an opportune moment to taste the progress of the wine. Occasionally, instead of using the long oak strips, I split the wine into smaller volumes and treat with either oak granules or the small chips. All methods have given good wines, but I favour the use of oak shavings during the pulp fermentation, followed by maturation with the long oak strips. However, it pays to have some unoaked wine, which can be blended with the oaked wine, if it is felt that the oaking has been overdone.

For white wines, I find the small oak chips and Gervin oak granules are better than oak shavings or the long oak strips. Oak shavings are rather rough on the white wines, and it easier to control the maturation of white wines with the small chips than with the long strips. With the Gervin product, the fine texture of the oak and its large surface area lend themselves well to the oaking of white wines. Equilibrium of the oak extraction is well nigh reached in 24 hours. Thus, if dealing with a wine made only from fruit juices, the oak granules would be added for 2 days sometime towards the end of the fermentation. As the optimum oak to wine ratio will vary for each particular wine, I think it is worth looking at the approach of the commercial world to oaking white wines. Often, only a fraction of the wine is oaked, and then blended with unoaked wine to find the best percentage of oak to suit that particular wine. Amateur white wines can be treated similarly. If two similar white wines are made, one oaked and one unoaked, they can then be blended to determine the perfect balance of oak to wine. Once determined, this amount of oak can be used in future batches of wine made to the same recipe. Therefore, I would suggest using 10g of Gervin granules to one gallon of wine, but initially to oak only a portion of the wine.

The small oak chips are also very successful in the maturation of white wines. Again, only a portion of the wine needs to be oaked in early experiments. I find that it is best to oak some of the wine using a ratio of 2 chips per litre of wine. Oak maturation in this way will need at least a month to show the relevant characteristics. Some of the richer styles of white wine, particularly attempts at Chardonnay, benefit greatly from the use of small oak chips, and these wines can often stand longer oaking of up to 3 months. As discussed with the Gervin granules above, the oaked wine can then be blended with the unoaked wine to find out the best balance.

The show bench has many good examples of wines whose exposure to oak have given them commercial-type characteristics, helping to close any gap that may exist between amateur and commercial wines. Oaked wines are commercial styles that are very common, with wine shelves in the supermarkets and high street stores filled with wines labelled as 'Oak-Aged', 'Barrel-Fermented', 'Lightly-Oaked', or similar expressions. Red oaked wines can be very smooth and velvety. Amateur winemakers should have no hesitation in using oak to improve the quality of their wines.

# eleven
# WHEN THINGS GO WRONG

## Hazes

There is little more frustrating in winemaking than a wine that is reluctant to clear. Even after taking all the precautions of adding bentonite and pectolase, a small percentage of wines remain cloudy. Often this cloudiness is in the form of a faint haze caused by colloidal particles held in suspension. The main hazes in wines are due to pectin, protein or very fine particles from the fruits used. Other hazes occasionally encountered are due to starch, gums and waxes, bacteria, and metals. Although the wine may have been treated with pectolase, the enzyme may have lost its activity in storage. Likewise, even after treatment with bentonite, protein from yeast autolysis may have appeared after racking. Tests exist for these various hazes, but even if one identifies the problem, the haze still has to be removed by treating with pectolase or using a fining reagent. By testing, on a small scale, the effect of a variety of fining agents on the wine, the winemaker is then in a position to scale up any fining method that is successful. The following is a selection of small-scale fining methods that, in my experience, have been successful in deducing the best clarifying agent for a particular wine.

## Isinglass

This is usually purchased as a concentrated suspension requiring about 10ml (0.35fl oz) for one gallon of wine. For the small scale test, dilute the isinglass 1 part in 10, say 0.5fl oz isinglass plus 4.5fl oz water. Mix 2.5ml (half a teaspoon) diluted suspension with 113ml (4fl oz) wine, and leave in a cool place. The wine should show definite signs of clearing within 24 hours if it is going to be successful.

## Two-part finings

This comes as two separate reagents, labelled A and B. A is silicic acid, and B is gelatine. The suggested doses are 1-2ml of each reagent for one gallon of wine. For the small-scale test, dilute both solutions 1 part in 100. Mix 5ml (one teaspoon) diluted reagent A with 100ml wine, leave for 30 minutes, then stir in 5ml diluted reagent B. Leave in a cool place. If successful, the wine should show definite signs of clearing within 24 hours.

## Bentonite

Bentonite is usually available as a dry powder, which has to be reconstituted to a 5% slurry with water. It is used at between 20ml and 100ml slurry per gallon of wine. For the small-scale test, make up a 1% slurry, mix 5ml (1 teaspoon) 1% slurry with 113ml (4fl oz) wine, and leave in a cool place. Again, the wine should be clearing within 24 hours if successful.

## Pectolase

If pectolase (pectolytic enzyme) has been used with the fruit before processing, or at the start of the fermentation, pectin should not be the cause of the haze. However, it easy to see if the addition of pectolase to the wine has any effect. The best source of pectolase used to be Gervin Supplies, which marketed the product as a tablet, which helped to prevent the loss of enzyme activity with time. Although the tablet product is no longer available, Boots the Chemists do a suitable alternative in powder form. For the small scale test, simply scale down the manufacturer's recommended dose, and leave at 20-25°C. If the haze is due to pectin, it will clear in 24 hours.

## Other fining reagents

Many of these exist, and here are a few of the more common.

**Egg white** is used mainly in fining red wines.

**Chitosan**, derived from crab and lobster shells, can be effective in clearing some stubborn hazes.

**Casein**, in addition to clarifying some hazy wines, can also reduce the colour in wines.

**Tannin** is often used along with gelatine to fine white wines.

Small-scale tests can be performed with these other fining reagents if the winemaker has a preference for any of them. If a fining reagent works on a small scale, the doses can be changed to find out the optimal dose for a particular wine. It may seem a fair amount of work, but once the diluted stocks of reagents are made the tests can be performed quickly and easily. Remember that there is little worse in winemaking than a persistent haze in a wine.

## Acetification

Acetification can appear as two compounds, acetic acid or ethyl acetate, both of which can be formed by different contaminating organisms. Fruit flies are a common source of bacteria that produce acetic acid, and many fruit skins carry wild yeasts capable of producing both acetic acid and ethyl acetate. There should be no problem in recognising wines or musts that have produced acetic acid, which is the pungent acid in vinegar. Ethyl acetate is an ester, which has a pleasant ethereal smell, something like pear-drops. Although contaminating organisms can produce both of these, ethyl acetate can also be found in old wines from the esterification of small amounts of acetic acid with ethyl alcohol. Unfortunately, there is little that can be done to save acetified wines. There is no reagent that is selective enough to remove these unwanted off flavours without being detrimental to the wine. I have tried volatilising off this volatile substance by treating the wine with solid carbon dioxide, but, although there was a noticeable reduction of the acetic problem in both bouquet and flavour, the wine had lost much of its fruitiness and vinosity. The only hope for such a wine is in the culinary department.

The answer to acetification is - don't let it happen. All equipment should be spotlessly clean. Even when equipment looks clean, the numbers of bacteria there can be very high, so imagine what a dirty container carries in the way of potential contamination. Often I see a winemaker's gallon jar or strainer with dirty pieces quite visible. Each of these can be carrying millions of contaminating bacteria and fungi. An overlooked source of contamination is the piece of tubing used to siphon wine from one vessel to another. Tubing is not easy to clean, but it can be done by filling the tubing with a cleaning solution and leaving it for some hours. Removal of stains in the inside of the tubing can be accomplished by squeezing the tubing along its entire length, rinsing well, and filling with sulphited water overnight. The golden rule is to clean everything immediately after use, to drain properly, and to store dry. The amateur cannot work under completely sterile conditions, but much can be done to approach such conditions. For example, gallon jars and fermentation bins that were stored clean and dry can be given a quick rinse with 1% metabisulphite before use. Throughout this book, I have advocated building up a large yeast starter for a variety of reasons. One of those reasons is that a large yeast colony will give virtually no chance for a contaminating organism to grow up in sufficient numbers to cause the winemaker any problem. In addition, starting with a large inoculum means that the alcohol content of the must will be high from an early stage. The wild yeasts cannot tolerate high-alcohol conditions, and few of the contaminating bacteria can survive above 10% alcohol.

## Butyric acid

This is hardly a common fault, but wines with taints of butyric acid do appear on the show bench. The cause is usually elderberries, especially dried elderberries. For some reason, elderberries appear to be very prone to harbouring bacteria that produce this insidious off flavour, somewhere between vile cheese and sweaty socks. This is why elderberries should be pasteurised before use. This is achieved by covering the elderberries with water, and heating beyond 80°C for 10 minutes, cooling immediately. This will kill all bacteria on the elderberries. Unfortunately, the damage can already have been done with dried elderberries, where the bacteria have been allowed to multiply during the drying process. If they are already contaminated with butyric acid, this will be evident by their smell. So sniff before you buy.

## Flowers of wine

There are a few strains of yeast that cause this infection, which can appear on the top of wines that have been racked and clarified. The reason that these yeasts stay on top of the wine as a thin film is that they use oxygen from the air space to break down the alcohol in the wine in order to obtain energy for survival. The quality of the wine is lowered in the process. There can little sympathy for winemakers who have this problem, as prevention is simple. When the wine is racked into a gallon jar, the jar should be filled to within a few millimetres of the top of the jar. Depending on the wine's history, between 1 and 5ml 10% metabisulphite should be carefully layered on top of the wine. The bottle should then be sealed with an airlock or other suitable closure that will not allow the access of air. Periodically, these jars should be examined. If the surface film appears, it should be removed immediately, and the wine treated with more metabisulphite immediately. But why store in gallon jars? When a wine is clear and stable, the best storage vessels are 2.5 litre bottles with Bakelite caps. These are used to hold industrial liquid chemicals, and are known as Winchesters. It is certainly worth trying to obtain some of these as they can be filled to the brim before sealing.

## Sulphur problems
Sulphur in the completed wine can present itself in a few forms. The sharp pungent smell of sulphur dioxide can be present in some wines, causing great difficulty in assessing the bouquet of the wine. This was often the case in commercial wines before modern winemaking equipment and techniques appeared on the scene. The problem was caused by excess use of sulphur dioxide to combat less than ideal winemaking conditions. The advent of new equipment such as stainless steel fermentation vessels, combined with more training in vinification technology, has led to less contamination, in turn reducing the amounts of sulphur dioxide used. Today, most commercial wines are fresh and clean, and seldom with any noticeable trace of offensive pungency. The amateur winemaker should learn from the commercial scene, as many show bench wines still suffer from the use of too much metabisulphite. In the chapter 'Winemaking Additives', the limited use of metabisulphite is discussed, showing that, by only using it on the fruits that matter, the amounts used can be lowered substantially. By taking great care to exclude oxygen during racking and fining, the amounts required at this stage of the vinification are also reduced. Other forms in which sulphur is encountered in the finished wine are as the smell of a burnt matchstick, or as the smell of rotten eggs. Both of these occur because the metabisulphite has reacted with other compounds in the must, or because it has been metabolised by yeast or bacteria. Whatever the reason, the more metabisulphite added the more likely these unwanted sulphur compounds are to appear.
Curing any of these problems is not easy. If metabisulphite is added to a wine, only a small portion will be lost to the atmosphere as volatilised sulphur dioxide. Therefore, the sulphur in the metabisulphite stays in the wine in one form or another. The sharp, pungent sulphur dioxide can be oxidised over a period of time, but dull sulphur overtones can still be detected in the background of the wine. It is reported that the smell of rotten eggs can be neutralised by the addition of metabisulphite, but there seems to be little point in adding yet more of an additive that is already causing a problem. Once again, the advice is the old adage 'prevention is better than cure'. If attention is paid to all steps of vinification, there should be no problems from sulphur faults in the wine. In the early stages, only the fruits require treatment with metabisulphite, added water, fruit juices, and concentrates being used as they are. Minimal exposure to air during racking and fining will also help to lower the amounts of metabisulphite that needs to be added during these later stages in the process.

## Mouse
Mouse is a dreaded infection in wine caused by a pyridine derivative produced by the action of bacteria or yeasts. It is detected as an aftertaste in the back of the throat. The French call such an unfavourable farewell the arrière goût. The unpleasant odour is released when the alkaline saliva in the palate causes the compound to volatilise into the nasal passage. The smell of mouse is not normally detectable in the bouquet of wines due to their high acidity, but, if made alkaline by the addition of sodium bicarbonate, the mousy smell is released and can be detected. This is the recognised test for suspect wines. Unfortunately, there is no cure that will still leave the wine in good condition. What would be required is

a product that would selectively remove the pyridine product. Such a product has yet to appear on the market. Yet again, the answer is - don't let it happen. The contaminants almost certainly appear early in the winemaking process, either through contaminated fruit or equipment, or careless vinification. This is another example of why working with a large yeast starter, and why sterilisation of the necessary fruits, can avoid infections. Exposure of the wine to air should also be kept to a minimum at all times.

## Geranium

The smell of geranium is produced when bacteria attack potassium sorbate, an additive used to stabilise sweet white wines. It can be avoided by the appropriate additions of sorbate along with metabisulphite, the latter being used to inhibit the bacterial attack. In the commercial wine industry, where some wines marketed as medium or sweet styles are treated with sorbate, the addition of metabisulphite is necessary to prevent the geranium off flavour being produced. However, I question the need for the use of sorbate in home winemaking. Although some amateur wines may have been designed to have various levels of sweetness, they can easily be stored dry until required. There is no difficulty in sweetening these up just before a wine show, or even just before some guests arrive. If the wine has been sweetened before, then the amount of the sweetener required is known, and the process can be carried out very quickly. Grape juice and grape concentrates are excellent ingredients for sweetening dry wines. Xylitol, an unfermentable sugar with sweetness very similar to sucrose, is a worthy candidate for sweetening wines that are planned for long-term storage.

## Oxidation

It is very difficult to oxidise wines that have started fermenting, especially if they have been set off with a large inoculum of yeast starter. This is because the yeast uses up all the dissolved oxygen, and fermentation produces a positive pressure of carbon dioxide that bubbles through the airlock. If the wine has been handled carefully, there will still be anaerobic conditions in the jar when the wine has finished fermenting. Careful racking, topping up with still wine or boiled water, and the addition of a modest amount of metabisulphite should retain these oxygen-free conditions. Similar care should be taken if the wine needs fining. Filtration is fraught with difficulties as far as oxidation is concerned, but speedy manipulations, lack of splashing, and a little ingenuity can usually produce a filtered wine free from obvious oxidation. Wines that are oxidised have not been well treated, and have little use other than being used as sherry styles, at least the white styles. However, as these wines were never designed to be sherries from the start, they seldom have the quality of well-made sherries. The oxidised sherry aroma is due to the formation of acetaldehyde by the oxidation of alcohol, a complete reversal of the last stage in the fermentation of sugar to alcohol. By adding the oxidised wine to a fermenting wine of similar style, the acetaldehyde can be reconverted to alcohol, removing most if not all of the sherry character. However, after so much heavy handling it would be asking a lot to expect a high-quality wine. Therefore, don't let oxidation happen.

## Stuck fermentations

This is a situation where the fermentation does not reach completion, often failing to reach a specific gravity of 1.000. There are many reasons for the early termination of some fermentations. Temperature affects the fermentation in two ways. When lower temperatures slow down the speed of fermentation, and sometimes bring it to a virtual halt, the fermentation usually restarts with no problems when the temperature rises. On the other hand, where rises in temperature to levels above 30°C occur, the fermentation not only ceases but also fails to restart when the temperature is lowered, due to the death of the yeast cells which will not survive long periods at elevated temperatures. Another reason for stuck fermentations is poor vinification techniques such as lack of sufficient nutrients, often found in flower wines and similar wines that use little diversity in fruit. Excess sulphur dioxide, stemming from liberal additions of metabisulphite, can also cause fungiostatic effects on wine yeasts. In the latter case, the wine is in little danger from bacterial attack, and should be re-fermentable with the introduction of a well-built-up yeast inoculum into the stuck ferment which will require sufficient aeration to neutralise the excess sulphur dioxide. In the wines where the stoppage has been due to temperature fluctuations or nutrient deficiency, the wine is in grave danger of spoilage due to bacterial attack on the residual sugar. In the absence of competition by the yeast cells, the bacteria will multiply and feed on the unfermented sugar source, leading to all sorts of off flavours such as mouse, lactic acid souring, and acetification. The fermentation should be monitored by the winemaker using specific gravity as a measure of its progress, with any stuck fermentation being treated immediately. The answer, of course, to avoid encountering this problem is to use sound yeast, to use a good mixture of fruit, to use the appropriate additions of nutrients, and to keep metabisulphite additions to a modest level.

## Re-fermentations

A wine that has finished fermentation, and has been racked and appears to be stable, will sometimes start re-fermenting after a period of time in storage. This re-fermentation is visible as bubbles of carbon dioxide, which can be seen rising to the top of the jar. This carbon dioxide is either coming from reactivated yeast, which is fermenting residual sugar in the wine, or from the metabolism of sugar or malic acid by lactic acid bacteria. The presence of sugar can be verified by checking the specific gravity, which should be below 0.995 if there is no residual sugar in the wine. If the specific gravity is higher than 0.995, there is almost certainly residual sugar, which could lead to contamination problems if the fermentation is due to bacteria. The wine yeast may have ceased activity due to temperature fluctuations or due to lack of nutrients. If the yeast is no longer active, and there is still residual sugar in the wine, the bacteria will have no competition from the yeast for the sugar. Normally, in the late stages of fermentation, there is an enormous yeast colony, and only very small numbers of lactic acid bacteria. It is not until the yeast has used up all the sugar that the bacteria start to multiply and, in the absence of sugar as an energy source, metabolise malic acid to lactic acid. However, in the presence of sugar and no yeast, the bacteria will use the sugar, producing off flavours such as mouse and lactic acid souring. The bacteria can be inhibited by a heavy dose of metabisulphite, 100-200ppm. If there is no sugar in the wine, the conversion of malic acid to lactic acid should be allowed to proceed, as the amounts produced will be insufficient to cause souring of the wine.

Nevertheless, the winemaker should have been following the progress of the fermentation, and been aware that the sugar had not all been used. At this stage the wine either has to be re-inoculated with a high-alcohol yeast strain and nutrients, or heavily sulphited to store as a non-dry wine.

## Poor extraction

Many less-experienced winemakers run into problems with poor extraction, especially in making red wines and after-dinner wines, wine styles that require pulp fermentations. The wines do not always appear to have the body or flavour that would have been anticipated from the ingredients in the recipe. For example, a gallon of after-dinner white wine may require 32oz sultanas, 8oz dates, 8oz figs, 8oz dried banana, 4oz dried rosehip shells, and 25fl oz white grape concentrate. There is sufficient sugar in those ingredients to produce over 18% alcohol. Although the wine may be made using good winemaking techniques such as building up the yeast starter in the white grape concentrate, and fermenting on the pulp for four days, the final wine can be rather thin with a lower alcohol level than would have been expected. Especially with dried fruit wines, there is a very high pulp-to-liquid ratio during the pulp fermentation. When the pulp is strained, the volume of spent pulp can be seen to be quite high, often about a third of the volume of the strained liquid, i.e., about one fourth of the total volume. However, the pulp is mainly liquid. If the pulp was dried out, the volume of the total solid pellet would be about 10% of the pulp volume. Thus, if the pulp is not re-extracted with more water, over 20% of the extraction will be lost. If, for example, 20% of the total possible extract is lost, the wine will have less than 15% alcohol, and its body, acidity, and flavour will be correspondingly reduced. The answer to this problem is to conduct the pulp extraction at a total volume of 8 pints, which should give about 6 pints of liquid when strained. The spent pulp should then be remixed with 2 pints water, and strained again to remove the liquid trapped in interstitial spaces in the pulp. After all, the beermakers sparge, why shouldn't the winemakers?

### In general
The take-home message for all these faults is "Don't let them happen". If the wine is treated with tender loving care all the way from the priming of the yeast right up to the final bottling, the problems above will not appear. Few experienced winemakers ever have to face these problems. If they do, they know that it was almost certainly operator error.

# twelve
# THE COMMERCIAL
# AS A STANDARD

It is not my purpose here to give examples of commercial wines, as readers will have their own preferences. However, I think that it is worth noting that few countries are blessed with such a selection of good wines from all over the world as is Britain, albeit that they tend to be more expensive here than elsewhere. The advent of supermarket wines and friendlier high street stores has increased sales and awareness of these wines. I think that all amateurs making their own wines have become more involved in the commercial world. This is hardly surprising, as commercial wines have to be the most suitable standard against which to compare our home-made wines. But how do our wines compare with commercial wines? I always think it is sad that when home-made wine is offered to guests not involved with amateur winemaking, the reception is often quite cold, as if they were struggling to say something complimentary about the wine. Compare this with offering them a piece of granny's home-made apple pie, where their minds immediately conjure up gastronomic delights better than the Roux brothers can produce. Are our wines really below the standard of commercial wines? Both the amateur and the commercial world make the following five wine styles. I will give my opinion of how the amateur matches up to the commercial in each of these styles.

## Dry White Table Wine

In general, this is one of the poorest classes that the amateur winemaker produces. One possible reason for this is that, apart from fresh or frozen grapes, there are not all that many suitable ingredients from which to make dry white wines of the calibre of the commercial. The best commercial dry white wines are made from the free-run juice from white grapes, or occasionally from the free-run juice from red-skinned grapes whose juice is white. Thus, skin contact is kept to a minimum, yielding wines that are fresh and clean in the palate, with no astringency in the aftertaste. More than any other trait in the wines, it is this clean freshness and lack of astringency in commercial wines that distinguish them from most amateur wines. Whether the amateur wines have been made from grapes or from a blend of other suitable ingredients, the juice usually has been allowed to have excess skin contact during a pulp fermentation, allowing harshness and bitterness to be extracted from the skins and seeds. This problem can be overcome by only using the juice run off from the fruits used, although a delay of 1-2 hours before separating the juice from the skins and seeds can prove beneficial to these wines. However, many of the non-grape white fruits have very strong flavours, and should be used in judicious proportions. Another option, of course, is to use commercially-available fruit juices, although these should be tasted first to ensure that that they are good quality and lack astringency and bitterness.

What do we find on the show bench? Certainly, Dry White Table Wine can be one of the hardest classes to judge. After the inevitable down pointing of wines due to faults such as excess sulphite, astringent aftertastes, and residual sweetness, the judge so often finds there is a selection of clean wines, few of which have any outstanding features. Most wines sell themselves on bouquet, a feature that is difficult to achieve in amateur Dry White Wines without resulting in strong harsh flavours in the wine, although much of this can be overcome by heeding the advice in the previous paragraph. Fortunately, at the top end there are usually one or two wines that have been given the tender loving care necessary for this style.

How do the wines in a Dry White Table class compare with their commercial counterparts? I find that commercial dry white wines have become better over the recent years with the advent of stainless steel fermentation, increased temperature control, and sensible use of mild oaking. The stainless steel fermentation vessel makes cleaning and sterilisation of winemaking equipment much easier and automation of the winemaking process allows for racking and transfer of wine with minimal exposure to oxygen, thus reducing the need for sulphur dioxide treatment at almost every stage of the process. Gone are the wines suffering from excess sulphur dioxide on the bouquet, or the wines spoiled by the oxidised form of the same product. From this, what the amateur has to learn is that cleanliness is an essential in all aspects of winemaking. The more care that the winemaker takes at all times reduces the amounts of sulphite required. The less sulphite that is added to a wine, the less sulphur there will be in the final product. They've learned it commercially, let us put it into practice in the amateur world. Temperature control during fermentation and storage has been a major factor in the improvement of dry white wines from places such as Spain, Australia, and California. These fresher, cleaner styles have dominated the market, replacing their dull, tired predecessors. We should learn from this, and consider fermenting our white wines at lower temperatures, as there are suitable yeasts available for fermenting down to temperatures below 10°C.

I think that there is definitely a gap between the standard of the average amateur and commercial wine Dry White Table Wine, but I feel that this gap can be closed if the amateur achieves better selection and handling of ingredients. Also, limiting the use of sulphite, and fermenting at lower temperatures, will lead to cleaner and fresher wines, which retain more of the bouquet of the ingredients. As frequently mentioned elsewhere in this book, the late addition of some of the ingredients can greatly enhance the bouquet and flavour of these Dry White Table Wines.

## Dry Red Table Wines

With such a selection of red indigenous fruits, concentrates, and bottled or tinned fruit, there can be no excuse for the amateur in this style. I find that there are two main failings, not only in the amateur scene but also commercially. Both these faults result from tannin. A percentage of both amateur and commercial wines are quite unapproachable due to excesses of harsh tannins. Even keeping these wines is not the answer, as many of them are tired and have lost their fruitiness by the time that the tannin drops to acceptable levels. The other problem arises when the wines have been made with short skin contact in order to reduce the amount of tannin in the wine. In achieving this, however, the wines are generally thin and low in fruit for this style wine. Although these are common failings in some amateur wines, these failings are also found in commercial wines. Similarly, as we go up in class in both amateur and commercial wines, we find that the amateur wines compare very favourably with commercial red wines in the middle price range. At the top end of an amateur Dry Red Table Wine Class we find wines that would grace any dinner table. The best of these wines have usually been made by sensible blends of red fruits and concentrates, red grape concentrate being an ingredient that has proven to be very suitable as a backbone for red wines. Based on these observations, my opinion is that amateur Dry Red Table Wines are generally well-made wines that compete well with the lower and middle priced end of the commercial Dry Red Table Wines. However, in order to compete with the more expensive red wines available, I feel that much more attention needs to be given to the making of heavier style dry red wines which require longer maturation, generally in oak.

## Rosé

Commercial rosés vary from dry to medium in terms of sweetness. These wines, somewhat underrated, can be excellent refreshing drinks in Britain's long and balmy summer. This is a style that the amateur can make very well, although the best wines are made from recipes designed to produce rosÈs from the start, rather than blends of red and white wines just before a wine show. These wines are usually at their best when young, fresh, and crisp.

## Sweet White Table Wines

Commercially, few sweet white wines are available at costs below £10.00, and few showing real quality are available under £20.00. I once tried to put on a wine tasting of modestly priced sweet white wines, and started to run out of ideas after a Spanish Muscatel, a Première Côtes de Bordeaux, and a South African Muscat. In the chapter 'Recipe Design', the development of a recipe to produce a Sauternes-style wine is described. This wine is not Chateau d'Yquem, but its consistency at winning first prizes in sweet white wine classes is very good. At one major show where there is a Sauternes class, the judge who is lucky enough to be given the class always praises the standard, in the judge's report on the result sheet. There can be little doubt that this is one style where the amateur makes wines that compare very well with the commercial counterpart, and at a fraction of the price.

### After-dinner Wines

Who was responsible for changing that marvellous description Dessert Wine? There are few examples of unfortified commercial After-dinner Wines. Most are not only fortified, but have also gone through processes to which few amateur wines are likely to be subjected. Madeira is fortified and virtually cooked at temperatures upwards of 37°C for up to six months, while port is little more than grapes marinated in distilled spirits. Again, to find real quality in these style wines, means digging deep into the pocket. Yet it is here that the amateur excels. I have tasted after-dinner style wines that would rival many expensive wines available commercially. When one considers that this has been achieved only by natural fermentation, it is even more commendable.

How close then are amateur home-made wines to the commercial? Can we easily tell them apart? One way to do this is to set up a blind tasting where the audience has to tell whether a wine is amateur or commercial. In order to do this each person has to taste something like ten wines in order to prove if the wines have been recognised properly. The selection of the wines is best done completely randomly by tossing a coin to select whether each wine, in turn, will be amateur or commercial. The wines are then served in clear competition bottles into which either the amateur or commercial wine has been decanted. I have organised one such tasting with five tasters and ten wines. Without boring readers with the results and the statistics involved, suffice to say that the results clearly showed that the group was not significantly successful in deciding if the wines were amateur or commercial. The commercial wines chosen were all in the £4.00-£6.00 range, and the styles chosen were sparkling, dry white, dry red, and after-dinner. The commercials can always be upgraded to wines in the £10.00-£20.00 range to see if the amateur winemaker can still compete at this level.

There is no doubt that the commercial is still the best standard we have, but my experiences at the show bench indicate to me that, certainly at the upper end of a wine class, amateur wines compete favourably in quality when compared to commercial wines. I think that we can be very content with the standards that have been achieved in home winemaking so far, but there is always room for improvement, particularly in the Dry White Table Wines.

# thirteen
# WINE CLUBS & WINE TALKS

Although this chapter describes only wine clubs, most clubs have a dual role in wine and beer. Wine clubs have to be the backbone of amateur home winemaking. However, before discussing their important place in home winemaking, let us have a look at the structure nationally in England. The governing body is The National Guild of Wine and Beermakers (NAWB) whose main object is to promote the art of home wine and beermaking. Membership of the Association is open to (a) individuals, (b) wine and/or beer circles, and (c) federations of wine and/or beer circles. It is sad that not all federations are affiliated to NAWB, and sadder still that only a fraction of wine circles will pay a minimal sum to become members, £10.00 at the time of writing. As far as individual membership is concerned, it is hard to understand how anyone truly interested in home wine and/or beermaking could not wish to become a member. Three very informative 'News and Views' magazines are sent free each year to members, and the membership fee is refunded to those who attend the social events at the yearly National Show.

Most of the wine clubs were formed in the sixties when home wine and beermaking was in its growth period. Although numbers are now dwindling over the years, we must keep the clubs flourishing, as they are the most important piece of the whole structure from the members through to NAWB. How can young people be persuaded to join a Wine Club? I feel confident that they would be extremely interested in joining the club if they were given an interesting social evening tasting good home-made wines, while also being instructed in the techniques of winemaking. It is essential that the wine clubs have a programme with a sensible wine subject each club evening. Too often, the clubs veer away from the very theme for which they were formed, with speakers talking on subjects not even remotely concerned with winemaking. Over the years, I have developed some interesting wine talks, which have always been well received. I will describe two of these, one on amateur wines and one on commercial wines, in enough detail that the talks could easily be organised by one or two club members.

**Are we doing it right? A talk on amateur winemaking**
The highlights of this talk have already been discussed in the chapter 'Ingredients and How To Use Them'. Here I want to describe the events that demonstrated that this approach made good sense. The first time that I involved other people in testing my theories for improving amateur winemaking was in High Wycombe just over ten years ago. At that time, in addition to the normal club evening, I used to organise a meeting once a month for a group who were more enthusiastic than the average club member. I had not given any information on the structure of my talk-cum-tasting. I opened with a brief resume of amateur wine making to date and queried "Where do we go from here?". After the definitive works of Acton and Duncan, the more recent excellent books by Gerry Fowles, and Gerry's eagerly awaited quarterly magazine, Wine For All Seasons, was there really much more that could be done to improve the efforts of the amateur winemaker? I explained to the group that the wines on the show bench gave us the answer, showing that much needs to be done to improve the quality of a high percentage of the competitors' wines. Although the top wines in a class were usually of quality high enough to earn respect when compared to well-rated commercial wines of similar style, the middle to bottom end had many wines that would have been marked higher if they had only been given more care and attention. But what care and attention should we be giving these wines over and above all that has already been described in great detail in many winemaking books? I stated that I felt that there were substantial improvements that we could make and that exploring these improvements was the purpose of the evening.

At this stage, I moved on to the more interesting aspect of tasting. I passed round two dry red wines, A and B, and asked for comments on the quality of the two wines. I have listed a few of the comments from my audience that evening.

"Wine A is much fruitier than wine B."

"Wine B has much harsher tannins."

"Wine A has a fresher, younger bouquet."

"Wine B appears to be tired and stale."

Clearly, the consensus of opinion was that wine A was by far the better wine, although we had one dissenter - isn't there one in every club? Agreeing that we were all (well - almost all) in favour of wine A, the next question was to determine why wine A was superior. The comments were interesting, and logical deductions from interpretations of the tasting.

"Wine A had more fruit to the gallon."

"Wine B is stale and tired - over the hill - much older."

"Wine B was made from elderberries, and Wine A from blackberries and blackcurrants."

"Wine A has higher acidity."

"Wine A has residual sweetness."

"They were made using different yeasts."

There were other similar replies, all reflecting that wine A was a very acceptable, very quaffable wine that would not be far away from awards on the show bench. Our dissenter said that he preferred wine B because he liked his red wines dry. I am sure that he confuses, as do many, richness with sweetness in a wine. As I had predicted that this discussion over apparent residual sweetness would occur, I had armed myself with a hydrometer and showed that both wines had the same specific gravity. We all agreed that wine A was rich and fruity and that wine B was austere and astringent. The 'extra' dryness he was experiencing in wine B was due to the astringency of harsh tannins, thus giving the impression that wine A was sweeter than wine B. This drying out, puckering sensation of the palate, is another area that causes confusion among many tasters of dry red wines. As my audience all wanted to know the difference in the two wines by now, I revealed all by reading out the ingredients used for Wine A, followed by the ingredients for·wine B.

| | Wine A | Wine B |
|---|---|---|
| Red grape concentrate | 16fl oz | 16fl oz |
| Blackberries | 8oz | 8oz |
| Blackcurrants | 8oz | 8oz |
| Elderberries | 8oz | 8oz |
| Raspberries | 8oz | 8oz |
| Bananas | 4oz | 4oz |
| Sugar | 19oz | 19oz |

As I had read these recipes out, it took some time for them to realise that the wines were made from identical ingredients. I further confused the issue by stating that both wines were started at the same time with the same yeast inoculum split equally between the two wines. Other suggestions that there was a difference due to one wine being oaked, or that one wine had been fined with isinglass or chitin, were also dispelled. So what was the difference? What could I have done to the same ingredients to produce such a change in two wines? I explained the difference in construction of the two wines to my audience, while presenting my reasoning for the improved quality of wine A.

Wine B was made by what are recognised standard winemaking techniques. Namely, 20fl oz yeast starter was made up by adding a sachet of Gervin varietal C to 4fl oz red grape concentrate and 16fl oz water. After allowing the starter to build up overnight, the red fruits were pasteurised in 1 litre of water by being taken just to the boil, cooled immediately, and homogenised along with the banana using a potato masher. After pectolase treatment, the pulp was transferred to a fermenting bin along with the rest of the grape concentrate, 3 pints of water, and 10fl oz yeast starter, the other half of the culture being used for wine A. After two days, the sugar was added and the fermentation on the pulp was allowed to continue for a further two days, four days on the pulp in total. The wine was then strained through a sieve into a demijohn, the spent pulp lightly sparged (rinsed through) with 20fl oz water, and the wine allowed to ferment to dryness. Standard racking procedures were performed when the fermentation was complete. The stabilised wine was stored for two months before the tasting.

And what of wine A? At the same time as starting the pulp fermentation for wine B, 10fl oz yeast inoculum was added to 14fl oz red grape concentrate plus 4 pints water, making the total red grape concentrate up to the 16fl oz required in the recipe. This was fermented in a demijohn adding the sugar in two stages, at three days and six days. A careful check was kept on the specific gravity and, when below 1.010, the red fruits were pasteurised, homogenised with the banana exactly as for wine B, and fermented on the pulp with the wine from the demijohn. The residual sugar was completely fermented out within the four day pulp fermentation. The wine was racked, the pulp sparged, and the wine moved on to stabilisation as for Wine B. Wine A was finished and racked about two days before Wine B.

The only difference between the making of the two wines was that Wine B had the fruit added at the start of the fermentation while Wine A had the fruit added very late in the fermentation. Although Wine B had been made using good winemaking techniques, the results of the tasting indicated that Wine A was the better wine. By adding the fruit very late in wine A, the freshness and richness of the ingredients had been preserved. This may seem to be obvious, but yet the vast majority of wines by far are made by pulp fermenting the fruit as the first step in making the wine. What are the reasons for this? Firstly, the instructions in winemaking books recommend this procedure. Furthermore, often little planning by the winemaker has gone into the timing of making a wine. Elderberries and other red fruits are picked and the decision to make a dry red or dessert-style wine is taken. Fruit sterilisation and yeast priming are initiated at the same time. The long lag phase for the yeast to multiply and use up the dissolved oxygen in the must can only encourage contamination and the eventual production of unpleasant flavours in the finished product. When fermentation finally takes off, the initial surge can be quite tumultuous, blasting lovely aromas into the room. How marvellous some kitchens smell when wine is fermenting! But it's not in the atmosphere that we wish these aromas to be - it's in the wine! Even during the subsequent anaerobic fermentation, which can last one to two weeks or even longer, the aromatics of the wine are volatilised into the atmosphere by the carbon dioxide produced during the conversion of sugar to ethanol. Surely this is not what we want? Surely we can do better? Let us examine the advantages of adding the fruit late, as in Wine A.

The tasting clearly showed that wine A had retained the freshness of the fruit while wine B had not only lost the fruity aromas of the ingredients but also, in addition, had harsher tannins. By the time these tannins in wine B had mellowed, there would be little quality left in the wine. It is relatively easy to see why the aromas and flavours of the red fruits in wine A had been preserved by adding them very late in the fermentation, but why did we also have softer, smoother tannins by this late extraction of the fruit? My reasoning is that, when the red fruit was added to wine A, the alcohol level was already well above 12%. Extraction of flavours, colours, and tannins at this high alcohol concentration is very fast, apparently releasing the tannins in an aggregated form that is very acceptable to the palate. These soft chewy tannins are normally only produced after long maturations which encourage the harsher monomeric tannins to aggregate with time.

A second advantage is that, by adding the fruit so late in the fermentation when the alcohol level is already well above 12%, the chances of a rogue contaminant growing is far less than in a normal fermentation where the yeast is added to the must in a fermentation bin. In the latter case, there is still abundant oxygen, which is a requisite for many of the contaminating organisms we normally run across in winemaking. On the other hand, with the late addition of fruit, all the dissolved oxygen has been used up in the early stages of the fermentation. The recently pasteurised fruit having been heated will contain little dissolved oxygen. After the transfer of the fruit to the fermenting grape concentrate and sugar, now with a large yeast colony in a high alcohol level, any dissolved oxygen will be used up in minutes rather than hours. This environment of high alcohol, minimal oxygen, and low pH, can only be described as extremely hostile to any invading organism. Furthermore, even if a contaminant that could survive under these conditions was introduced, it is most unlikely to multiply due the overwhelming competition for nutrients by the well-established yeast colony. So much so, that one could even question why it is necessary to bother with pasteurisation of the fruit at all. Certainly, I have often done this myself, simply adding in the mashed thawed fruit with no sterilisation precautions at this stage of the process. However, I hesitate to recommend this as a standard procedure in case any reader manages to cultivate bacteria, capable of surviving anaerobically in high alcohol conditions and producing undesirable off flavours.

I now gave my audience four wines labelled C, D, E, and F, and asked them to identify the dominant fruit from a choice of blackberry, blackcurrant, elderberry, or raspberry, indicating that, in my opinion, each one of those fruits was dominant in one of the four wines. I encouraged them to make their own decisions, and not to be swayed by know-it-all neighbours. After a suitable period of time, I recorded their votes. Out of 19 present, 14 voted C as blackberry, 17 voted D as blackcurrant, 12 voted E as elderberry, and 18 voted F as raspberry. When I revealed that all four wines were made using exactly the same ingredients, the audience, or at least the smarter ones, were beginning to see the plot. The recipe was identical to the one used for Wine A and Wine B. The twist was that, in Wine C, the blackcurrant, elderberry, and raspberry had been fermented first, as would have been done in wine B. Very, very late in the fermentation, after the wine had been strained, and slowing down of carbon dioxide production showed that there was minimal sugar left, an overnight pulp fermentation was done with the blackberries. This was then strained, made up to a gallon, and the wine completed with standard techniques. Wines D, E, and F were similarly treated, with blackcurrant, elderberry, and raspberry being the late-added fruit. The results clearly indicated that the late added fruits could be identified. Four people identified all four correctly, while the biggest confusion was over blackberry and elderberry. This was further evidence to my audience that, by fermenting the fruits early in the fermentation, quality was being lost in the wines. It can be difficult persuading people to change their habits and accept new ideas, but I know of at least four converts I made from that evening. This talk is always well received, and feedback I receive from winemakers who have adopted the approach of 'late fruiting' is always very encouraging.

### The wine memory, a memory test on commercial wines.

Tasting a range of commercial wines with a group of friends is an enjoyable way to spend an evening. Such evenings can be made extremely interesting and informative by tasting the wines blind. These tastings can also be organised for wine clubs, cutting down the costs involved as a bottle of wine will serve over 20 people for this purpose. The format of the tasting can be varied depending on the ability of the audience. A very popular blind tasting is to attempt to identify four different white wine grape varietals. For dry white wines, four very good choices are Sauvignon Blanc, Chardonnay, Gewürztraminer, and Muscat. In the £4.00 - £6.00 range, there are plenty of wines that would prove eminently suitable for a tasting like this. Examples readily available at the time of writing are Chilean Valdivieso Chardonnay, New Zealand Highfield Estate Sauvignon Blanc, Alsace Turckheim Gewürztraminer, and Portugal's Jao Pires Muscat, all £4.99-£5.49. The wines are then served one at a time, and evaluated by the tasters, who generally make notes, specifically trying to identify aspects of the wine which may help them to identify the wines later when they are tasted blind. Tasters can be helped by giving them tasting notes from other sources such as Jancis Robinson's Masterclass or the Taste Tunnel of Wine by the Sunday Times Wine Club. Each wine is discussed in turn for its quality and suitability as an example of its grape variety. When all four wines have been tasted, four competition bottles labelled A, B, C, and D are then produced. The tasters are asked to pour themselves a glass of each wine, and identify the grape variety of each wine. These are, of course, the same wines rebottled and labelled in random order. All four wines can be poured into four separate glasses for each taster, giving them a chance to taste and retaste before making a final decision.

Although the exercise appears straightforward and relatively easy; few people manage to identify all four wines correctly, and it is not unusual in an audience of over 30 to find that nobody has identified all four wines. By random guessing, there is a 1 in 24 chance of having all four correct, and 6 in 24, 8 in 24, and 9 in 24 of having 2, 1, or 0 correct. Of course if anyone has three correct, then they must have all four correct. By performing statistics on the results, it is fairly easy to show if there is any significance in the ability of the tasters to identify the grape varieties. Most clubs thoroughly enjoy this exercise which can be modified depending on the ability of the members. When tasted for the first time, the bottle labels can be covered, introducing a more difficult task for the more skilled winemakers who will have to identify unknown grape varieties. The rest of the evening then proceeds as above. The game can also be played with red wines, sweet white wines, and dessert style wines. If skills are extremely high and these are all too easy, four Chardonnays from different countries can be selected for the evening. All these alternatives are marvellous ways to spend an evening tasting good quality wines, while introducing some interest and education to the evening.

Here are outlines of other interesting wine subjects that I have presented over the years.

### Sparkling wines
The full process of making sparkling wines is discussed, with practical examples of wines at various stages of the process, including live examples of disgorging - wise club members do not take a front seat. Tastings are provided of five sparkling wines that have all been made from the same basic still wine.

### A versatile wine
This concept has been described in the chapter with the same title. Starting from a wine of about 16% alcohol, five competition-standard wines are produced by blending in sight of the audience. The five wines are appraised for their suitability on the show bench, and many winemakers appear keen to use this approach to blending for shows.

### Five wines for a dinner
Five wines, suitable for a dinner party are served. The wines have all been made from typical amateur winemaking ingredients. Each recipe is discussed in detail as the wines are tasted. This talk demonstrates how a dinner party can successfully be held with minimum costs involved.

### After-dinner wines
Five after-dinner wines, from very simple to more complex recipes, are tasted and discussed. The design of the recipes is discussed, along with the beneficial use of oak in these style wines. Home winemakers can excel in making these styles, as is demonstrated in the tastings provided.

### Wines to a recipe
The audience is shown how a recipe to produce a commercial-style wine was developed over a period of time by tasting the initial effort, by the development of different ideas into the recipes, all the way to the final recipe. The audience compares the final wine with the commercial that was chosen as the standard throughout the development of the recipe. The development of recipes is discussed further in the chapter Recipe Design.

### Amateur or commercial
Can we tell the difference between an amateur wine and a commercial wine? The audience are given a blind tasting of wines which could be amateur or commercial. This talk is described in more detail in the chapter The Commercial as a Standard, but, as yet, no group has shown significant ability in being able to tell amateur from commercial.

# fourteen
# WINE SHOWS
# AND COMPETITIONS

There is a whole spectrum of wine shows, all the way from the small village hall to the National. The local wine shows are often part of the village horticultural show, attracting entries from the once-a-year competitor who manages to avoid all attempts to be ensnared into the local wine club. The wine classes at these shows are often few in number, with the rules somewhat lax, and are often judged by unqualified judges. A move up from the village show takes us to the larger district and county shows that are generally judged by local members of The National Guild of Wine and Beer Judges. These shows can be very interesting as they often have classes reflecting the traditional country-wine styles. Federation shows are extremely well organised, often with some of the officials being National Judges. The Convener of Judges organises a team of National Judges, most of who live locally. The standard of these shows can be very high, as some of the competitors compete at National level. Then, of course, there is the National Show itself, the year's biggest event. Recently, the National Show has been sited alternately at Weston-super-Mare and Scarborough. The weekend is excellent, with the competition, wine tastings, social events on Friday and Saturday nights, and the AGM on Sunday morning after a guest speaker.

The highlight of all these shows is the wine and beer competition, organised as a series of classes, each an example of a typical wine or beer class. In the wine section, most shows will cover all the table-wine styles, with additions such as fruit and flower classes, and with some class entries confined to wines from concentrates. No two schedules for a show are the same, all adding to the attraction of one particular show. Entering a show for the first time can be somewhat daunting, especially having to decide the classes in which to enter various wines. Some schedules have more than one class in which a single wine could be entered.

The first requirement is to read the schedule. This may sound elementary, but many competitors fail to achieve this necessary task. The first and most obvious guidance to be obtained from the schedule is the date and venue of the show. On numerous occasions I've heard the same story - "Oh, is it this weekend? It's too late to enter now." Although these competitors may not be the most enthusiastic winemakers in the area concerned, they often constitute the backbone of the wine clubs, and the shows concerned need their entries.

In addition to instructions for labelling, corking, and delivery of entries, the schedule will also offer advice on the styles of wines in the various competition classes. Mandates need to be obeyed. For example, if the schedule states that the wine in an apple class may only be made from apples, sugar, with the necessary yeast, nutrients, finings, and stabilising agents, then it is illegal to enter a wine made from apples plus other fruits or concentrates. On the other hand, where the schedule is vague, use it to your advantage. An excellent example would be a class described as red grape concentrate sweet, where the schedule states that the wine may only be made from red grape concentrate and sugar with the other necessities already mentioned. It is unlikely that the winemaker will make anything approaching an adequate After-dinner Red Wine from one 26fl oz can of concentrate plus the necessary sugar. However, if one and a half cans of concentrate are used, the wine takes on a different complexion, especially if oaked during fermentation and/or maturation. Yet this wine would have been made to the specifications in the schedule, which did not stipulate that the wine had to be made to manufacturer's instructions, and which did not ban the use of oak. Any competitor who is in any doubt about schedule rules should contact the Convener of Judges for the show and ask for counsel. After all, it is the Convener of Judges who will have to make the final judgement on the acceptability of any doubtful entry. Here is some advice on the main classes found in shows, based on my experiences as competitor and judge.

### Three bottle class

Here the competitor has to produce three different styles of wine, usually Dry White Table Wine, Dry Red Table Wine, and After-dinner Wine. Often a competitor will enter an experimental bottle of wine to gain information from the judge's comments. The three bottle class is no place to do this, as one poor bottle will ruin the selection. Some shows even have a five bottle class to challenge enthusiastic competitors. This is generally the three styles already mentioned with the addition of a Dry Aperitif and a Sweet White Table Wine. Again, controversial wines should be avoided, as five good sound wines will be hard to beat.

### Table, White Dry
Attractive bouquets and light, fresh, clean styles are the answer here. As long pulp fermentations inevitably produce astringency and bitterness in these wines, skin contact should be kept to a minimum. Suitable ingredients are fresh grapes and fruit juices, including grape juice. If strong-flavoured fruits are used, the amounts should be minimal. When bone dry, these wines can be austere, and will be improved by the addition of 30ml white grape juice per competition bottle. This will soften the wine in the palate, without giving the wine perceptible sweetness.

### Table, White Medium
Like the Table, White Dry, this should be fresh and clean, and free from astringency. The bouquet should be encouraging, with floral styles often prevalent. Although there can be a wide range of sweetness from the sweet side of medium dry to the dry side of medium sweet, the sweeter wines usually do better, provided that they are in good balance. Given that the choice of ingredients has produced good flavours in the wine, the secret here is the balance of sweetness, acidity, and alcohol. White grape juice and white grape concentrates are excellent ingredients for honing this balance.

### Table, White Sweet
This style can be more robust, and benefits from the addition of small amounts of honey and aromatic fruits. As these wines are usually very sweet, the acidity can be surprisingly high to balance the sweetness and alcohol which can be as high as 14%.

### Table, Red Dry
Fruitiness, smoothness, and lack of excess astringency from harsh tannins are the key to this wine. Oaking during the pulp fermentation and/or the maturation of the wine is very beneficial, giving the soft velvety characteristic associated with well-matured red wines. However, the oaking should be well judged and should not hide the fruitiness of the wine.

### Table, Rosé
The schedule usually indicates whether the wine should be dry, medium dry, or medium. The best wines are those designed to be rosés from the outset, these wines most often proving to be superior in quality to last-minute blends of white and red wines.

### After-dinner Wines
Generally, the heavy, high-alcohol wines do best here. The white styles, described in most shows as 'After-Dinner Wine White to Brown', often have very high acidities to balance the sweetness and alcohol. Madeira is a good example of a commercial style whose sweet wines carry around 20% alcohol, and acidities of 0.7-0.9%. When well oaked, these wines are very smooth in the palate. The red styles can have a little less sweetness and acidity, and also benefit greatly from good oaking.

### Fruit Wines
If an individual fruit is named, that fruit must dominate the wine to such an extent that there is little doubt that the wine was made from it. Where no fruit is named, the better wines are usually mixtures of fruit, adding complexity to the bouquet and flavour. If oak is used, it must be kept to a minimum to avoid masking the fruitiness of the wine.

**Flower Wines**

It is essential to have a floral bouquet, which should be clean and attractive. Elderflowers and rose petals are eminently suitable for this role. The wine is generally light in style, with the floral characteristics dominating any other ingredients.

There are many other wines encountered in various shows whose schedules often give helpful advice on the different styles.

On the day of the show, as the judges arrive for their duties, entries will have been received and laid out neatly under their class headings. About an hour after judging commences, the results start rolling in, a hectic time for the Show Secretary and helpers. Soon it is all over, with lunch and speeches, and later the prizegiving. The competitors collect their bottles, complete with a comment card for each bottle, and head off home. So is it all over for the competitor? Not if he or she wishes to improve. Assuming that the competitor has entered 12 bottles, these will be accompanied by 12 comment cards. In my experience, these comments are usually very informative, giving the judge's opinion of the wine and reasons for its positive or negative values. Our competitor should, either the same day or the following day, taste each of the wines, comparing the wine with the judge's written comments. Almost invariably the comments will prove to be sound, giving helpful information to the competitor. This inquest is something that I always carry out on my own wines - it pays to be humble. It is lovely to gloat over a wine that won a first prize, but what of the other wines that I thought were excellent but failed to make the grade? So often the judge will detect a flaw that I had not detected in my own wine. Tasting the wine again usually leaves me in full agreement with the judge, and thankful that such wines, whether made by me or others, are not likely to sneak past the vigilance of National Judges. If done seriously, such an exercise builds up more information in the wine memory, making preparation of wines for future shows much easier.

# fifteen
# A SELECTION OF RECIPES

This chapter contains a selection of recipes covering ten of the wine styles encountered. These recipes have been formulated either by myself, by Chilterns Masters, or by winemaking friends. The designer of each recipe has been acknowledged. All the recipes assume good winemaking techniques, such as the appropriate use of nutrients, metabisulphite, and pectolase. These should be used according to manufacturers' instructions, although the advantage of using metabisulphite and pectolase on only the fruits requiring treatment has been discussed in the chapter 'Ingredients and How to Use Them'. Where no specific advice on the pectolase addition has been given, this should be added with the fruits. Where necessary, advice has been given on individual fruits. Where the wine will benefit from manipulations such as late-added fruit, this has been mentioned in the recipe. All recipes are for one gallon (4.54 litres), but do note that most gallon jars contain nearer to 5 litres when full. A useful tip is to increase all the ingredients by 10%, which allows for the larger gallon jar, and also allows for volume losses during racking. This use of 10% extra fruit means that the gallon jar can be full, thus eliminating any air space that would encourage oxidation and contamination of the wine. Some of the amounts used in these recipes may seem strange, but this is due to scaling down of some of the recipes from 4.5 or 5 gallons to 1 gallon. All the alcohol levels quoted are as a percentage by volume, and the acidities are based on tartaric acid as the reference standard. The acidity values quoted are estimated from the acids in the ingredients used in the recipes. The final titratable acidities may be different, depending on the fermentation conditions and the balance of the different fruit acids. Final adjustment of the acidity can be done as described in the chapter 'Winemaking Additives'.

Many of the recipes to follow advocate 'building up the yeast starter' before tackling the preparation of the fruit. As discussed in the chapter 'Ingredients and How to Use Them', this allows fermentation with the fruit to start with a large pure yeast culture which will inhibit growth of contaminating organisms in the must. Advice on racking, sulphiting, fining, and filtering has not been given for these individual wines as this has been covered in the chapter 'From Racking to Bottling'.

All the yeasts suggested for the recipes are Gervin yeasts, available from most home winemaking retailers.

## Dry Aperitif Wines

There are three main commercial styles of aperitif. These are oxidised wines such as sherry, herbal wines such as vermouth, and bitter wines such as Punt e Mes. The alcohol content of most of these aperitif wines can vary from 14-17%, with some of the fortified sherries having up to 21%. There can be a range of sweetness in these wines, but the recipe examples given are all dry, as these are more suited to the purpose of aperitif wines; stimulation of the appetite. Apart from the heavier fortified wines such as Madeira and Oloroso sherry, aperitif wines are light in style. In addition to these styles, amateur winemaking has produced a citrus-style, which has no commercial equivalent. In making citrus style wines, choice of ingredients should be restricted to those that will impart the qualities of freshness and zest.

**Dry Aperitif Wine: Grapefruit**
*from 'Wine Recipes for the Connoisseur' by Ted Adcock*

| | | |
|---|---|---|
| Grapefruit juice | 35fl oz | 1 litre |
| White grape concentrate | 12fl oz | 340ml |
| Apple juice | 17fl oz | 500ml |
| Sugar | 23oz | 652g |
| Nutrient | | |
| Pectolase | | |
| Yeast: Gervin no. 6 | | |

This is an amateur wine style with no commercial equivalent. The use of citrus fruits produces fresh clean wines with a little zest, ideal for an aperitif. This recipe has been designed to produce 14% alcohol and an acidity of 0.6 %.
Build up the yeast with the diluted white grape concentrate and sugar to a volume of 6 pints. When most of the sugar has been used, add the grapefruit juice and apple juice and ferment to dryness. Rack and clarify using standard techniques. The wine needs to mature for at least a year to show its best qualities.

**Dry Aperitif Wine: Citrus Style**
*from 'Winemaking in Style' by Gerry Fowles*

| | | |
|---|---|---|
| Grapefruit juice | 11fl oz | 300ml |
| Pineapple juice | 14fl oz | 400ml |
| Dried dates | 4oz | 100g |
| White grape concentrate | 9fl oz | 250ml |
| Sugar | 28oz | 800g |
| Gervin maturing solution | 0.2fl oz | 5ml |
| Nutrients | | |
| Pectolase | | |
| Yeast: Gervin no. 1 | | |

The recipe should give an alcohol content of 15%, and a final acidity not exceeding 0.5%. Build up the yeast starter with the diluted grape concentrate and sugar to a volume of 5 pints. When most of the sugar has been used, mash the pasteurised dates, add the fruit juices, and treat with pectolase for 4 hours. Ferment on the pulp for 2 days. Strain into a gallon jar, top up with boiled water, and ferment to dryness. Rack and clarify by standard techniques. The wine produced is quite complex, relying on the grapefruit for its aperitif character.

**Dry Aperitif Wine: Orange Style**
*by Anne Mills, Harrow Guild of Winemakers*

| | | |
|---|---|---|
| White grape concentrate | 10fl oz | 284ml |
| Tinned shredded Seville oranges | 28oz | 794g |
| Bananas | 10oz | 284g |
| Sugar | 25oz | 709g |
| Tartaric acid | 0.4oz | 11g |
| Pectolase | | |
| Nutrients | | |
| Yeast: Gervin no. 3 | | |

Build up the yeast starter with the diluted white grape concentrate. Liquidise the bananas and put them in a small fermentation bin along with the shredded oranges. Add pectolase and metabisulphite to 100ppm, and leave for 24 hours. Add the dissolved sugar, tartaric acid, and yeast starter, making the total volume up to 8 pints. Cover, and ferment on the pulp for 7 days. Strain into a gallon jar, top up, and ferment to dryness. Rack and fine using standard techniques. This wine, with about 14% alcohol and 0.6% acid, should be ready for drinking in 6 months.

### Dry Sherry Wine: Fino Style
by *Bill Smith*

| | | |
|---|---|---|
| White grape juice | 35fl oz | 1 litre |
| Vine prunings, frozen fresh shoots | 16oz | 454g |
| Rhubarb, chopped and frozen | 16oz | 454g |
| Victoria plums | 32oz | 907g |
| Sugar | 35oz | 992g |
| Pectolase | | |
| Nutrients | | |
| Yeast: Gervin varietal C | | |

The secret with vine prunings is to pre-freeze the prunings, crush them while still frozen, and extract them overnight by just covering with cold sulphited water. This avoids the harsh greenness that is found if the fresh prunings are extracted with hot water.

Build up the yeast starter with the white grape juice. Thaw the chopped frozen rhubarb, and strain off the juice, pressing very lightly, and adding 100ppm metabisulphite. Combine the rhubarb and vine pruning extracts, treat with pectolase, and add half the sugar along with the yeast starter. After 2 days, wash the plums in hot water with a few drops of detergent. This will remove the unwanted waxes and gums found on plums. Remove the skins at this stage, and rinse well to remove all traces of detergent. Destone the plums, mash the flesh, treat with pectolase, and ferment on the pulp for 24 hours. Strain into a gallon jar, adding the rest of the sugar. Top up with water, and ferment to dryness. Rack and clarify using standard techniques, but do not top up the gallon jar after racking. This is to allow some modest oxidation of the wine. The wine should be inspected regularly, and racked into smaller containers when the required degree of oxidation has been achieved. At this stage, the containers should be well sealed with no air space. Mature for at least 9 months. This fino style should have about 15% alcohol and 0.5% acidity.

### Dry Aperitif Wine: Vermouth Style
by *Bill Smith*

| | | |
|---|---|---|
| White grape juice | 70fl oz | 2 litres |
| Apple juice | 35fl oz | 1 litre |
| Bananas | 4oz | 113g |
| Sugar | 28oz | 794g |
| Gervin vermouth essence | 0.6oz | 17ml |
| Pectolase | | |
| Nutrients | | |
| Yeast: Gervin no. 6, strain 8906 | | |

Start the yeast culture with the white grape juice and apple juice. After 4 days, mash the banana, and pulp ferment overnight. Strain into a gallon jar, add the dissolved sugar, and top up the gallon jar.

Ferment to dryness, racking and clarifying using standard techniques. When the wine is clear, make up a stock of the vermouth essence by adding 17ml to 1 pint of the wine. This stock then can be mixed with a portion of the rest of the wine to produce the Vermouth strength required. This will produce a clean, fresh, low acid vermouth-style wine with about 16% alcohol. If necessary, raise the acidity slightly as described in the chapter 'Winemaking Additives'.

## Dry White Table Wines

There is a whole range of commercial styles of dry white table wines, which used to be described by the area from which the wines came e.g. Burgundy, Bordeaux. More recently, these wines have come to be recognised by the grape variety from which they are made e.g. Chardonnay, Sauvignon Blanc. The alcohol content of these wines can vary from 8-14%, although most tend to be in the 11-13% bracket. The acidity can be from 0.5% to as high as 0.8%, giving the wines a clean and fresh farewell.

To make these style wines, consideration should be given to conducting the fermentation at temperatures around 15°C. These wines are best made from fruit juices, keeping pulp fermentations to a minimum.

### Dry White Table Wine: Burgundy Style
*from 'Winemaking in Style' by Gerry Fowles*

| | | |
|---|---|---|
| Apple juice | 70fl oz | 2 litres |
| White grape juice | 35fl oz | 1 litre |
| Pineapple juice | 7fl oz | 200ml |
| Gooseberries, frozen | 16oz | 454g |
| Bananas (flesh) | 4oz | 100g |
| Oak granules | 1 teaspoon | 1-2g |
| Nutrients | | |
| Pectolase | | |
| Yeast: Gervin varietal D | | |

Build up the yeast starter with the grape juice. Thaw the frozen gooseberries by pouring boiling water over them and, when cool, break the skins by squeezing them between finger and thumb. Add the mashed banana flesh and pectolase, and leave for 4 hours. Press the mixture to extract as much juice as possible, straining into a gallon jar along with the other juices and the yeast starter. Top up the gallon jar with boiled water, and ferment to dryness. On the first racking, add the oak granules. Further rack and clarify using standard techniques. The full bodied wine should show complex character, with 13% alcohol and 0.7% acid. The addition of a little passion fruit, or juice containing passion fruit, can enhance this wine.

### Dry White Table Wine: Sauvignon Blanc Style
*by Chilterns Masters*

| | | |
|---|---|---|
| White grape juice | 70fl oz | 2 litres |
| Apple juice | 35fl oz | 1 litre |
| White grape concentrate | 16fl oz | 455ml |
| Bananas | 4oz | 113g |
| Bottled or tinned gooseberries | 22oz | 624g |
| Sugar | 4oz | 113g |
| Nutrients | | |
| Pectolase | | |
| Yeast: Gervin no. 2, strain Davis 522 | | |

Build up the yeast starter to a volume of 6 pints in a gallon jar with the white grape concentrate, white grape juice, and sugar. When most of the sugar has been used, mash the banana and gooseberry in the apple juice; treat with metabisulphite and pectolase overnight, and pulp ferment with the rest of the ingredients for 2 hours. Strain into the gallon jar, rinsing the pulp with water to top up the gallon jar. Ferment to dryness, racking and clarifying by standard procedures. This recipe gives a dry crisp wine, true to Sauvignon Blanc style, with 13% alcohol and acidity between 0.6% and 0.7%.

### Dry White Table Wine: Chardonnay Style
*by Chilterns Masters*

| | | |
|---|---|---|
| White grape concentrate | 20fl oz | 568ml |
| Bananas | 4oz | 113g |
| Mangos | 8oz | 227g |
| Peaches | 4oz | 113g |
| Guavas | 4oz | 113g |
| Sugar | 16oz | 454g |
| Tartaric acid | 0.4oz | 11g |
| Gervin oak granules | as required | |
| Nutrients | | |
| Pectolase | | |
| Yeast: Gervin no. 2, strain Davis 522 | | |

Build up the yeast starter to a volume of 6 pints in a gallon jar with the white grape concentrate and sugar. When most of the sugar has been used, mash the other fruits; treat with metabisulphite and pectolase overnight, and pulp ferment with the fermenting white grape concentrate for 2 hours. Strain into the gallon jar, rinsing the pulp with water to top up the gallon jar. Ferment to dryness, racking and clarifying by standard procedures. With the completed wine, it is worth oaking a litre of the wine with 5g oak granules for 24 hours. This may be slightly over oaked but can easily be blended with the unoaked wine to produce the required degree of oakiness. This Chardonnay style will have an alcohol content of about 13%, and the acidity should be between 0.5% and 0.6%.

## Dry White Table Wine: Muscadet Sur Lie Style
*by Alan Thurlow, Harrow Guild of Winemakers*

| | | |
|---|---|---|
| White grape juice | 35fl oz | 1 litre |
| Apple juice | 35fl oz | 1 litre |
| Greengages | 16oz | 454g |
| Whitecurrants | 12oz | 340g |
| Sugar | 23oz | 652g |
| Tartaric acid | 0.1oz | 3g |
| Pectolase | | |
| Nutrients | | |
| Bentonite | | |
| Yeast: Gervin varietal D | | |

This recipe is designed to produce a fresh dry wine with 12-13% alcohol and 0.5% acidity.
After removing the stones from the greengages, mash the pulp along with the whitecurrants. Ferment on the pulp for up to 48 hours using all the sugar and boiled, cooled water at a volume of 6 pints. Strain into a gallon jar; add the grape juice, the apple juice, and half the tartaric acid. Ferment to a specific gravity of 1.005, taste for acidity, and add more tartaric acid if necessary. When fermentation is complete, the specific gravity should be between 0.990 and 0.992. Rack into a fresh gallon jar; leave for 48 hours, then fine with two part finings. Without further racking, leave for 8 weeks, giving a stir every week to encourage contact between the settled yeast cells and the clearing wine. Rack and clarify by standard techniques, and bottle when clear and stable.

## Dry White Table Wine: Hock Style
*by Vic Hallows, Federation of Chilterns and Mid Thames Wine Guilds*

| | | |
|---|---|---|
| White grape concentrate | 12fl oz | 341ml |
| Rhubarb | 8oz | 227g |
| Sultanas | 12oz | 340g |
| Bananas | 4oz | 113g |
| Honey | 8oz | 227g |
| Sugar | 8oz | 227g |
| Tartaric acid | 0.2oz | 5g |
| Elderflower, lightly packed | 5fl oz | 142ml |
| Pectolase | | |
| Nutrients | | |
| Yeast: Gervin varietal D | | |

Both the white grape concentrate and the honey should be as light a colour as possible. Start up the yeast in diluted grape concentrate and sugar in a volume of 4 pints. When most of the sugar has been fermented, thaw the chopped and frozen rhubarb, and strain the juice with a very light pressing. Homogenise the sultanas, and add to the rhubarb juice and the pasteurised honey. Treat with pectolase, and add the yeast starter. Ferment on the pulp overnight, and strain into a gallon jar to a volume of 7 pints. When the specific gravity has fallen to 1.000, add the elderflower, and allow to soak overnight. Strain into another gallon jar, and top up with water. Ferment to dryness, racking and clarifying using standard techniques. Although the wine drinks well as a dry style, with an alcohol content of 12% and an acidity of about 0.5%, a range of interesting wines can be made by sweetening with white grape juice or white grape concentrate.

### Medium Dry to Medium White Table Wines

The medium dry styles have just enough sweetness to be perceptible without this being a dominant part of the wine. They should also be light in style, generally with low alcohol and fairly high acidity. The most common examples of the medium dry style are German wines. German wines continue to be found as medium styles, fairly similar to the medium dry, but with a little more sugar and body. Medium wines carrying more alcohol and body are to be found from Bordeaux and the Loire. The alcohol levels usually range from 8-13%, with some of the acidities as high as 0.9%.

Again, low temperature fermentations are advantageous, and fruit juices are preferable to pulp fermentations. The German styles benefit from the use of elderflower to give characteristic floral bouquets.

### Medium Dry White Table Wine: Sainsbury's Montlouis Style
by John Holgate, Harrow Guild of Winemakers

| | | |
|---|---|---|
| Pure Cox apple juice | 26.5oz | 750ml |
| Pure Bramley apple juice | 26.5oz | 750ml |
| White grape juice | 70.5oz | 2000ml |
| Five Alive mixed citrus | 17.7oz | 500ml |
| Sugar | 8oz | 227g |
| Pectolase | | |
| Nutrients | | |
| Yeast: Gervin no. 2 | | |

This medium dry wine is very pale in colour, with a pronounced bouquet and flavour of apples. The bouquet in particular also has overtones of citrus fruit and melons. The alcohol should be about 11%, and the acidity is not prominent at 0.6%.

Build up the yeast starter with some of the white grape juice. Dissolve the sugar in the fruit juices, and put all the ingredients in a demijohn with the additives and the yeast. When the initial burst of fermentation is over, make up to 1 gallon with boiled water, and ferment to dryness. When racked and clear, add metabisulphite at 50ppm. Fine with potassium caseinate, which may help to reduce the colour. Sweeten to specific gravity 1.002 with a non-fermentable sweetener such as xylitol.

**Medium Dry White Table Wine: Moselle Style**
*by Bill Smith*

| | | |
|---|---|---|
| White grape juice | 35fl oz | 1 litre |
| Rhubarb, chopped & frozen | 16oz | 454g |
| Vine prunings; frozen fresh shoots | 32oz | 907g |
| Sugar | 24oz | 680g |
| Tartaric acid | 0.5oz | 14g |
| Fresh elderflowers, lightly packed | 20fl oz (2 cups) | 568ml |
| Pectolase | | |
| Nutrients | | |
| Yeast: Gervin D, strain 71B | | |

This recipe makes an elegant white wine with a pale colour and a delightful floral vinous bouquet. The secret with vine prunings is to pre-freeze the prunings in a plastic carrier bag, crush the prunings while still frozen, and extract them in cold water. This avoids the harsh greenness that is found if the fresh prunings are extracted with hot water. The chopped rhubarb should also be pre-frozen in plastic bags. The fermentation should be carried out below 20ºC.

Build up the yeast starter with the white grape juice. This should be timed for about 10 days before the elderflowers are picked. Crush the vine prunings while still in the plastic bag. Stamping on the bag is a good way to achieve this. Transfer to a bin along with the frozen rhubarb chunks, cover them with cold water, add enough metabisulphite to give 100ppm, and leave overnight to diffuse. Strain the vine prunings and rhubarb into a gallon jar, give the residue a quick rinse with about a pint of water, and strain again. Add the sugar, acid, and yeast starter, and ferment at a volume of 7 pints. When the specific gravity is about 1.000, add the fresh elderflowers to 2 pints of the fermenting wine, add metabisulphite to 100ppm, and leave for 1 hour. Strain back into the gallon jar, top up with water, and ferment to dryness. After racking and clarifying, the wine should be dry with an alcohol content of about 11% and acidity between 0.6% and 0.7%. The wine drinks best as a medium dry style, and this is easily achieved by sweetening with white grape juice to taste, usually about specific gravity 1.000.

**Medium Dry White Table Wine: German Style**
*by Bill Smith*

| | | |
|---|---|---|
| White grape juice | 70fl oz | 2 litres |
| Apple juice | 18fl oz | 500ml |
| Rhubarb, chopped & frozen | 18oz | 500g |
| Honey | 5oz | 142g |
| Sugar | 14oz | 397g |
| Tartaric acid | 0.25oz | 7g |
| Pectolase | | |
| Nutrients | | |
| Yeast: Gervin D, strain 71B | | |

Start the yeast culture with the white grape juice. On day two place the pre-frozen chopped rhubarb in 1 litre of sulphited water. Strain the rhubarb, pressing lightly, add the apple juice and the pasteurised honey, and treat with pectolase. After 2 hours add these to the fermenting grape juice, add the sugar and acid, and ferment to dryness at a temperature below 20ºC. Rack and clarify using standard techniques. When clear, now with an alcohol content of 11% and an acidity of 0.7%, sweeten to taste with between 50ml and 100ml white grape juice to 1 litre of wine, adjusting the acidity if necessary. The recipe makes a very acceptable and interesting German-style wine, which changes in character with the addition of up to 1 pint of fresh elderflower florets, marinated into the final wine.

## Medium White Table Wine
*by Sandra Claydon, Downley Wine Circle*

| | | |
|---|---|---|
| White grape juice | 70fl oz | 2 litres |
| Apple juice | 35fl oz | 1 litre |
| Tinned peaches | 8oz | 227g |
| Tinned lychees | 8oz | 227g |
| Sugar | 14oz | 397g |
| Tartaric acid | 0.4oz | 11g |
| Nutrients | | |
| Pectolase | | |
| Yeast: Gervin no. 5 | | |

The apples should be a mixture of ripe eating and cooking apples, from which the juice should be pressed or steam extracted.

Build up the yeast starter with the grape juice, apple juice, acid, and sugar to a volume of 5 pints. When most of the sugar has been used, crush the peaches and lychees, treat with pectolase and metabisulphite, and pulp ferment for 2 days. Strain into a gallon jar, top up with water, and ferment to dryness. When racked and clarified, sweeten to taste, specific gravity approximately 1.015. The final sweetened wine will have an alcohol content between 10% and 11%, with an acidity of about 0.7%.

## Medium White Table Wine
*by Jack Tunmore, Harrow Guild of Winemakers*

| | | |
|---|---|---|
| White grape juice | 35fl oz | 1 litre |
| Apple juice | 35fl oz | 1 litre |
| Honey | 4oz | 113g |
| Tinned peaches | 22oz | 624g |
| Bananas | 8oz | 227g |
| Sugar | 13oz | 369g |
| Tartaric acid | 0.4oz | 11g |
| Bentonite | 0.2oz | 5g |
| Nutrients | | |
| Pectolase | | |
| Yeast: Gervin varietal C | | |

Build up the yeast starter with the white grape juice. Pour the apple juice, pasteurised honey, and sugar into a fermentation bin and add the pectolase, nutrient, bentonite, and acid. Stir well, and leave for 12 hours. Add the yeast starter, and ferment for 2 days. Mash the bananas and peaches, and add to the fermentation with enough water to make 1 gallon. Ferment for a further 4 days, and then strain into a demijohn. Top up the jar, and ferment to dryness. Rack and clarify using standard techniques. When clear, stabilise by adding 1 Gervin potassium sorbate tablet and 5ml 10% metabisulphite. Sweetening to taste, usually about specific gravity 1.010, should give a wine with 10% alcohol and 0.6% acidity.

## Sweet White Table Wines

The most notable feature of commercial sweet white table wines, is that good ones are not cheap. This is partly due to the immense care and attention that has to be given to working with late picked grapes. Some of these wines can be very rich, with deep golden colours. The alcohol can be up to 14%, with high acidities of 0.6-0.9% to balance the high levels of sweetness.

The amateur winemaker makes good sweet white table wines, many of the ingredients used blending well to give complex flavours similar to the commercial styles. Balance of the completed wine is all important, usually requiring acidity adjustments to counter the high sweetness of the wine.

### Sweet White Table Wine: Sauternes Style
*by Chilterns Masters*

| | | |
|---|---|---|
| White grape concentrate | 13fl oz | 369ml |
| Apple juice | 35fl oz | 1 litre |
| Glycerol | 2fl oz | 57ml |
| Rhubarb, chopped & frozen | 32oz | 907g |
| Clover honey | 8oz | 227g |
| Strawberries | 4oz | 113g |
| Sugar | 21oz | 595g |
| Nutrients | | |
| Pectolase | | |
| Yeast: Gervin no. 6, strain 8906 | | |

The development of this recipe has been discussed in the chapter 'Recipe Design'. Build up the yeast starter with the apple juice. Thaw the frozen chunks of rhubarb, and press lightly through a sieve to extract the juice. Treat the juice with pectolase and metabisulphite, add the white grape concentrate and sugar, and ferment at a volume of 5 pints. When most of the sugar has been used, pasteurise the honey and strawberries, treat with pectolase, add the glycerol, and pulp ferment for 2 hours on the mashed strawberries. Strain, make up to 1 gallon, and ferment to dryness. When clear, sweeten to a specific gravity of about 1.020 with sugar, then round off the balance with white grape juice or white grape concentrate, usually to a specific gravity of about 1.030. Although this wine is very approachable as soon as it is made, it improves remarkably in the first year. Mild oaking has also been used to good effect in this wine. Depending on how the wine is sweetened, the final alcohol will be between 13% and 15%, with an acidity between 0.6% and 0.7%.

**Sweet White Table Wine: Sauternes Style**
*from 'Wine Recipes for the Connoisseur' by Ted Adcock*

| | | |
|---|---|---|
| White grape juice | 70fl oz | 2 litres |
| Gooseberries | 32oz | 907g |
| Bananas | 16oz | 454g |
| Honey | 16oz | 454g |
| Sugar | 14oz | 397g |
| Glycerol | 2fl oz | 57g |
| Pectolase | | |
| Nutrients | | |
| Yeast: Gervin no. 5 | | |

The best results are achieved with this wine when the gooseberries are as ripe as possible. Build up the yeast starter with the white grape concentrate over a period of 2 days. Liquidise the gooseberries and bananas, and treat with pectolase and metabisulphite. Ferment on the pulp overnight, and strain into a gallon jar, adding the pasteurised, pectolase-treated honey. Add the sugar and top up the gallon jar. After racking and clarification, add the glycerol. To ensure stability, add one tablet of Gervin potassium sorbate, along with the correct amount of metabisulphite. The dry wine has 16% alcohol and 0.7% acidity, but these values will be lowered when sweetened. The wine benefits from a short maturation which softens its texture on the palate.

**Sweet White Table Wine**
*by John Holgate, Harrow Guild of Winemakers*

| | | |
|---|---|---|
| White grape concentrate | 12fl oz | 340ml |
| Flower honey | 8.8oz | 250g |
| Rhubarb, chopped, frozen | 16oz | 450g |
| Tinned peaches | 92oz | 2600g |
| Tinned strawberries | 4.4oz | 125g |
| Sugar | 12oz | 340g |
| Tartaric acid | 0.2oz | 5g |
| Sorbate | 1 tablet | 1 tablet |
| Nutrients | | |
| Pectolase | | |
| Yeast: Gervin varietal E, strain K1 | | |

This recipe has been designed for 5 litres of wine, and is suitable for using in a gallon jar as most gallon jars contain almost 5 litres when full to the brim. Build up the yeast starter with the diluted white grape juice. Thaw the chopped, frozen rhubarb, strain out all the juice, and treat with metabisulphite and pectolase. Liquidise the peaches and strawberries, and transfer to a fermenting bin along with the pasteurised honey, sugar, and tartaric acid. Add the yeast starter, make up to just less than 5 litres, and ferment on the pulp for 2 days. Strain into a gallon jar, top up, and ferment to dryness. When fermentation is finished, rack carefully, and add 10ml of 10% metabisulphite and the sorbate tablet in order to stabilise the wine. When the wine is clear and stabilised, sweeten to taste. The sweetened wine will be between 13% and 14% alcohol, with an acidity level of 0.5% to 0.6%.

**Sweet White Table Wine**
*by Bill Smith*

| | | |
|---|---|---|
| White grape juice | 70fl oz | 2 litres |
| Apple juice | 35fl oz | 1 litre |
| Rhubarb, chopped & frozen | 16oz | 454g |
| Honey | 4oz | 113g |
| Nectarines | 16oz | 454g |
| Lychee flesh | 4oz | 113g |
| Strawberries | 4oz | 113g |
| Sugar | 16oz | 454g |
| Pectolase | | |
| Nutrients | | |
| Yeast: Gervin no. 6, strain 8906 | | |

Build up the yeast starter with the white grape juice. Thaw the chopped, frozen rhubarb by covering with sulphited water. Strain off the juice, pressing very lightly. Treat the rhubarb and apple juice with pectolase, and add to the yeast starter along with the sugar and pasteurised honey. When most of the sugar has been used, blanch the nectarines and remove the skins and stones. Mash the nectarines, lychees, and strawberries, treat with pectolase, and ferment on the pulp overnight. Strain into a gallon jar, top up with water and ferment to dryness. Rack and clarify using standard techniques. The wine should be stored dry at its alcohol content of about 15%, and its acidity content of 0.7%. It can be sweetened to taste, usually about specific gravity 1.030, with sugar, white grape concentrate, or white grape juice. This selection of sweeteners gives a range of sweet white wines that can be produced from the same recipe.

**Sweet White Table Wine**
*by Bill Smith*

| | | |
|---|---|---|
| White grape juice | 35fl oz | 1 litre |
| Gooseberries, frozen | 32oz | 907g |
| Rhubarb, chopped & frozen | 8oz | 227g |
| Nectarines | 48oz | 1361g |
| Strawberries | 4oz | 113g |
| Honey | 4oz | 113g |
| Sugar | 24oz | 680g |
| Pectolase | | |
| Nutrients | | |
| Yeast: Gervin no. 6, strain 8906 | | |

Build up the yeast starter with the white grape juice. Thaw the chopped, frozen rhubarb, and strain off the juice, pressing lightly. Thaw the frozen gooseberries, mash them, add 2 pints water, and leave for 2 hours, stirring occasionally. Strain the juice into a gallon jar, along with the rhubarb juice and the pasteurised honey. Treat with pectolase and metabisulphite to 100ppm. After 4 hours, add the yeast starter and the sugar, making the volume up to 6 pints. Allow the fermentation to proceed, and, when most of the sugar has been used, blanch the strawberries and nectarines, removing the nectarine skins and stones in the process. Mash the fruit, treat with pectolase, add the contents of the gallon jar, and ferment on the pulp overnight. Strain into a gallon jar, and top up with water. Ferment to dryness, and rack and clarify using standard techniques. When stored dry, the wine should be about 15% alcohol, with an acidity level of about 0.8%. Slight variations of a sweet white table wine can be made by sweetening with sugar, white grape concentrate, white grape juice, or a mixture of these. Sweetening with elderflower grape concentrate or a range of fruit juices and concentrates can produce other interesting variations.

## Dry Red Table Wines

As with the dry white table wines, these wines are becoming recognised more and more by their grape varieties, with Cabernet Sauvignon and Tempranillo now rivalling Bordeaux Claret and Spanish Rioja for a place on the wine store shelves. These dry red wines can be complex and heavy, with noticeable astringency from tannins, although the tannins should be soft and velvety in the more mature wines. Alcohol ranges are usually 12-14%, with acidities between 0.45% and 0.65%.

In making these styles, the amateur winemaker should pulp ferment the red fruit. Grape concentrate is a useful backbone ingredient, and can be used to build up the yeast starter, allowing the winemaker to carry out the pulp fermentation much later in the vinification procedure. This allows the extraction of the fruit to be conducted at high alcohol

levels, facilitating extraction and lowering contamination problems.

### Dry Red Table Wine: Burgundy Style
*by Bill Smith*

| | | |
|---|---|---|
| Red grape concentrate | 8fl oz | 227ml |
| Elderberries | 16oz | 454g |
| Blackberries | 24oz | 680g |
| Raspberries | 2oz | 57g |
| Strawberries | 1oz | 28g |
| Dates | 5oz | 142g |
| Oak shavings | 1oz | 28g |
| Sugar | 13oz | 369g |
| Sultanas | 13oz | 369g |
| Pectolase | | |
| Nutrients | | |
| Yeast: Gervin no. 6, strain 8906 | | |

This wine is designed to give an alcohol content of 13%, and an acidity of 0.5-0.6%.
Build up the yeast starter with the diluted red grape concentrate and the sugar at volume of about 4 pints.
When most of the sugar has been used, pasteurise the elderberries, blackberries, dates, sultanas, and oak,

cooling immediately. Mash the pasteurised fruit, treat with pectolase for 4 hours, and ferment on the pulp for 2 days before adding the mashed raspberries and strawberries. Ferment on the pulp for only 2 more hours, stirring frequently. Strain into a gallon jar, rinse the pulp with water, and re-strain. Top up the gallon jar, and ferment to dryness. When clarified, put 2 strips of oak into the gallon jar and mature for 6 months, stirring monthly to aid maturation of the wine. The wine benefits from a further 6 months in bottle. The use of these oak strips has been described in the chapter 'Oak'.

## Dry Red Table Wine: Chianti Style
*by Chilterns Masters*

| | | |
|---|---|---|
| Red grape concentrate (Solvino) | 20fl oz | 568ml |
| Bottled Morello cherries | 16oz | 454g |
| Elderberries | 12oz | 340g |
| Raspberries | 2oz | 57g |
| Strawberries | 4oz | 113g |
| Sugar | 16oz | 454g |
| Oak shavings | 1oz | 28g |
| Nutrients | | |
| Pectolase | | |
| Yeast: Gervin No. 2, strain Davis 522 | | |

The development of this recipe, designed to produce a wine with 13% alcohol and 0.5% acidity, has been discussed in the chapter 'Recipe Design'. Build up the yeast starter with the red grape concentrate and sugar to a volume of about 5 pints. When most of the sugar has been used, pasteurise the elderberries, raspberries, strawberries, and oak. When cool, add the Morello cherries, mash, treat with pectolase, and pulp ferment for 2 days. Strain, rinse the pulp with water, restrain, make up to 1 gallon with water, and ferment to dryness. Rack and clarify using standard procedures. The wine will benefit from further oaking during maturation.

## Dry Red Table Wine: Barolo Style
*Ingredients from 'Wine Recipes for the Connoisseur' by Ted Adcock*

| | | |
|---|---|---|
| Elderberries | 48oz | 1380g |
| Blackberries | 32oz | 900g |
| Bananas | 16oz | 450g |
| Sugar | 26oz | 730g |
| Tannin | 0.1oz | 3g |
| Nutrients | | |
| Pectolase | | |
| Yeast: Gervin no.2, strain Davis 522 | | |

This recipe, made from indigenous red fruits and no grape concentrate, benefits tremendously from the addition of 1oz Gervin oak granules during the pulp fermentation. Start the yeast culture with a little sterile fruit juice. Homogenise the elderberries and blackberries, mash them along with the bananas, and treat with pectolase for 4 hours. Add the yeast starter and the dissolved sugar, and pulp ferment for 4 days at a volume of 7 pints. Strain into a gallon jar, and rinse the pulp with 1 pint of water. Top up the gallon jar, and ferment to dryness. Rack and clarify using standard techniques. The wine, with an alcohol level of 13% and an acidity of 0.5%, should be further oak matured for at least 9 months in order to reach its true potential.

### Dry Red Table Wine: Barolo Style
*by Alan Thurlow, Harrow Guild of Winemakers*

| | | |
|---|---|---|
| Blackberries | 76oz | 2154g |
| Strawberries | 16oz | 454g |
| Solvino red grape concentrate | 13fl oz | 369ml |
| Sugar | 20oz | 567g |
| Gervin oak granules | 0.8oz | 23g |
| Pectolase | | |
| Nutrients | | |
| Yeast: Gervin varietal A | | |

This recipe is designed to give an alcohol content of 13% and an acidity between 0.6% and 0.7%.
Build up the yeast starter with the red grape concentrate. Mash the blackberries, and ferment on the pulp for 4 days, using all the sugar at a volume of 6 pints. Add the liquidised strawberries, and ferment for a further 24 hours. Strain into a gallon jar, top up with water and ferment to dryness. Rack, and add the oak. When the wine is clear, allow to mature for a minimum of 6 months.

### Dry Red Table Wine: Claret Style
*by Vic Hallows, Federation of Chilterns and Mid Thames Wine Guilds*

| | | |
|---|---|---|
| Red grape concentrate | 20fl oz | 568ml |
| Blackcurrants | 8oz | 227g |
| Elderberries | 16oz | 454g |
| Bilberries | 16oz | 454g |
| Dried rosehip shells | 2oz | 57g |
| Bananas | 4oz | 113g |
| Sugar | 24oz | 680g |
| Pectolase | | |
| Nutrients | | |
| Yeast: Gervin no.2, strain Davis 522 | | |

Build up the yeast starter with diluted red grape concentrate, and pulp ferment for 2 days with the pasteurised mashed red fruit, banana, and rosehip shells in a volume of 6 pints. Strain into a gallon jar, add the sugar, and ferment to dryness. Rack and clarify using standard techniques. The wine, with a final alcohol level of 13% and an acidity of 0.5%, benefits from further oak maturation for 6-12 months.

### Dry Red Table Wine: Claret Style
*by Bill Smith*

| | | |
|---|---|---|
| Red grape concentrate | 20fl oz | 568g |
| Elderberries | 16oz | 454g |
| Blackberries | 16oz | 454g |
| Blackcurrants | 19oz | 539g |
| Raspberries | 3oz | 85g |
| Dried apricots | 3oz | 85g |
| Dates | 4oz | 113g |
| Lychee flesh | 2oz | 57g |
| Sultanas | 7oz | 198g |

| Sugar | 8oz | 227g |
|---|---|---|
| Oak shavings | 1oz | 28g |
| Calcium carbonate (chalk) | 0.25oz | 7g |
| Pectolase | | |
| Nutrients | | |
| Yeast: Gervin varietal E, strain K1 | | |

This wine, with an alcohol content of about 13% and an acidity between 0.5% and 0.6%, benefits from the use of many ingredients which add complexity to the wine. Only small amounts of powerful flavours such as lychee and raspberry are required to lift the aromas in the final wine. The high acidity of the ingredients has been lowered by the addition of calcium carbonate.

Build up the yeast starter for a week using the red grape concentrate and the sugar at a volume of 4 pints. Following this, pasteurise the elderberries, blackberries, dried apricots, dates, sultanas, and oak shavings, then cool, mash, and treat with pectolase. Add the yeast starter, and ferment on the pulp for 2 days. Pasteurise the blackcurrants and raspberries, mash along with the lychee flesh, and treat with pectolase. Add these fruits and the calcium carbonate, ferment on the pulp for another 24 hours, and strain into a gallon jar. Rinse the pulp with water, re-strain, top up the gallon jar, and ferment to dryness. Rack and clarify by standard procedures. When clear, mature further by adding 2 oak strips per gallon of wine, stirring monthly to aid maturation of the wine. The wine will improve when bottled for more than 12 months. The use of these oak strips has been discussed in the chapter 'Oak'.

## Rosé Table Wines

Commercially, these vary in sweetness from dry to medium sweet. There is also a wide range in colours from very pale onion skin through to deep pink. Light fruity styles prevail, with alcohol between 10% and 12%, and acidity from 0.55-0.9%.

The best rosés made by the amateur are those made from ingredients designed to produce a pink wine, rather than by blends of white and red wines. Small amounts of raspberry, redcurrant, and blackberry all give good pink colours and fruity bouquets.

### Rosé Table Wine: Tavel Style
*by Bill Smith*

| White grape juice | 70fl oz | 2 litres |
|---|---|---|
| Apple juice | 35fl oz | 1 litre |
| Blackberries | 16oz | 454g |
| Raspberries | 2oz | 57g |
| Nectarines | 4oz | 113g |
| Lychee flesh | 1oz | 28g |
| Sugar | 16oz | 454g |
| Pectolase | | |
| Nutrients | | |

Yeast: Gervin D, strain 71B

Build up the yeast starter with the white grape juice, the apple juice, and the sugar at a volume of 6 pints. When most of the sugar has been used, mash the solid fruit, and treat with pectolase and metabisulphite at 100ppm. Ferment on the pulp overnight, and strain into a gallon jar, topping up as necessary. Rack and clarify using standard techniques. The wine is best as a dry wine, with 13% alcohol and 0.6% acidity, although 40ml white grape juice per litre of the dry wine softens the wine in the palate without showing perceptible sweetness.

### Rosé Table Wine: Worcesterberry, Medium Dry
*by Bill Smith*

| | | |
|---|---|---|
| White grape juice | 50fl oz | 1.4 litres |
| Vine prunings, frozen fresh shoots | 16oz | 454g |
| Rhubarb, chopped & frozen | 8oz | 227g |
| Worcesterberries | 32oz | 907g |
| Lychee flesh | 1oz | 28g |
| Strawberries | 1oz | 28g |
| Nectarines | 8oz | 227g |
| Sugar | 21oz | 595g |
| Nutrients | | |
| Pectolase | | |
| Yeast: Gervin D, strain 71B | | |

Worcesterberry is a cross between blackcurrant and gooseberry, giving a berry with gooseberry flesh and a deep-coloured skin. The fruit makes a very lively, salmon pink rosé which always is well received on the show bench. Start the yeast culture in the white grape juice. Crush and soak the frozen vine prunings overnight in enough sulphited water to cover them, then strain through a sieve next day. Thaw the frozen chunks of rhubarb in sulphited water, and press lightly through a sieve to extract the juice. Add the yeast starter to the vine pruning and rhubarb extracts along with the sugar, making the volume up to 5 pints, and treating with pectolase. When most of the sugar has been used up, mash the rest of the fruit, and treat with pectolase and metabisulphite at 100ppm for 4 hours. Pulp ferment for 2 hours, then strain, make up to 1 gallon with water, and ferment to dryness. Rack and clarify by standard procedures. When finished, the wine drinks well as a medium dry style, and is best sweetened with white grape juice, giving a wine with 11-12% alcohol and an acidity about 0.7%.

### Rosé Table Wine : Medium
*by Chilterns Masters*

| | | |
|---|---|---|
| White grape juice | 35fl oz | 1 litre |
| Apple juice | 35fl oz | 1 litre |
| Rhubarb, chopped & frozen | 16oz | 454g |
| Blackberries | 16oz | 454g |
| Raspberries | 2oz | 57g |
| Sugar | 20oz | 567g |
| Nutrients | | |
| Pectolase | | |
| Yeast: Gervin D, strain 71B | | |

After thawing the frozen chunks of rhubarb, press lightly through a sieve to extract the juice, and treat with pectolase and metabisulphite. Start the yeast with the white grape juice, apple juice, rhubarb extract, pectolase, and sugar in a total volume of 5 pints. When most of the sugar has been used, pasteurise the raspberries and blackberries, and treat with pectolase. Ferment on the pulp for 2 hours. Strain, make up to 1 gallon with water, and ferment to dryness. Rack and clarify by standard procedures. This wine is best when young, drinking optimally as a medium style. The wine can be sweetened with either white grape juice or white grape concentrate, giving two slightly different medium rosés. Depending on the method of sweetening, the completed wine will be between 10% and 11% alcohol, and will have an acidity between 0.5 and 0.6%.

### Rosé Table Wine: Anjou Style, Medium
*by Alan Kimber, Harrow Guild of Winemakers*

| | | |
|---|---|---|
| Clarified apple juice | 70fl oz | 2 litres |
| Red grape juice | 30fl oz | 850ml |
| Cranberry juice | 17fl oz | 500ml |
| Sugar | 20oz | 567g |
| Tartaric or citric acid | 0.35oz | 10g |
| Bentonite | 0.2oz | 5g |
| Nutrients | | |
| Pectolase | | |
| Yeast: Gervin varietal C | | |

This recipe is designed to give a wine with 12% alcohol and an acidity of about 0.7%.
Build up the yeast starter with the apple juice and the grape juice. Dissolve the sugar and the acid in 1 litre of boiling water and, when cool, place in the fermenting jar. Add the activated yeast and the nutrients to the gallon jar, and fit an airlock to the jar. Two days after fermentation starts, add the bentonite (hydrated, if the common powdered variety is used). When fermentation has quietened down and there is no danger of foaming, add the cranberry juice, top up to 1 gallon, and allow fermentation to proceed to dryness. Rack, and sulphite with 10ml of 10% metabisulphite solution, fining as necessary. The wine must be sweetened to a specific gravity of 1.000. If xylitol is available for sweetening, this can be done at any time. If sucrose is used, the sweetening must either be done just before drinking or accompanied by a further 5ml of stock metabisulphite solution and a potassium sorbate tablet.

### Rosé Table Wine
*by Bill Smith*

| | | |
|---|---|---|
| White grape juice | 70fl oz | 2 litres |
| Redcurrants | 32oz | 907g |
| Raspberries | 4oz | 113g |
| Sugar | 19oz | 539g |
| Pectolase | | |
| Nutrients | | |

Start the yeast culture in the white grape juice, and ferment for 4 days. Mash the redcurrants and raspberries and treat with pectolase and metabisulphite to 100ppm. Add the dissolved sugar, and ferment on the pulp for 2 days, strain into a gallon jar, and rinse the pulp with a pint of water. Top up the gallon jar, and ferment to dryness. Rack and clarify using standard techniques. Although the wine drinks well as a dry wine, it is at its best as a medium dry style which should be sweetened to taste with white grape juice, 50-100ml to a litre of wine usually giving the required degree of sweetness. The wine should be between 11% and 12% alcohol, and should have an acidity around 0.7%.

## After-dinner Wine, White To Brown

The most common styles encountered commercially are fortified, and can contain up to 21% alcohol. Popular styles include Madeiras and Sherries, both of which can have very deep brown colours. The Madeiras in particular can have very high acidities, up to 0.9%. Less common, and very expensive, are unfortified wines made from late picked grapes, such as Trockenbeerenauslese styles with alcohol levels around 10%. These wines are seldom encountered on the amateur show bench.

Perhaps the wide range of dried fruit ingredients explains why the amateur does so well at making this style of wine. Dried ingredients such as dates, figs, sultanas, and rosehip shells give the depth of colour and flavours suitable for this style. With a good high-alcohol yeast and the necessary nutrients, high alcohol levels around 20% can be attained. Honing the final sugar, alcohol, and acidity balance is one of the secrets to succeeding with this wine.

## After-dinner Wine, White to Brown
from 'Home Winemaking the Right Way' by Ken Hawkins, published by Elliot Right Way Books

| White grape concentrate | 25fl oz | 710ml |
|---|---|---|
| Sultanas | 32oz | 907g |
| Dates | 8oz | 227g |
| Figs | 8oz | 227g |
| Dried bananas | 4oz | 113g |
| Citric acid | 0.2oz | 5g |
| Sugar | as much as possible | |
| Nutrients | | |
| Pectolase | | |
| Yeast: Gervin D, strain 71B | | |

Build up the yeast starter with diluted white grape concentrate. After 2 days, liquidise the washed sultanas, dates, and figs, and transfer to a fermenting bin. Chop the dried bananas, and boil for 25 minutes in 20fl oz water. Strain, and add the liquor to the fermenting bin, making the volume up to about 50fl oz with water. When cooled to 20°C, add 5ml 10% metabisulphite, the pectolase, and leave covered overnight. Add the acid, nutrients, and yeast starter, and ferment on the pulp for 4 days at a volume of about 7 pints.

Strain into a gallon jar, and continue the fermentation under an airlock, adding 4oz sugar each time the specific gravity falls below 1.010. After racking and clarification, sweeten to specific gravity 1.040, adjusting the acidity as required. The wine needs at least 6 months to reach its peak. The wine should have over 18% alcohol, with high acidity to balance the sweetness.

## After-dinner Wine, White to Brown: Bual Style
*by Bob Hawtin, Booker Wine Circle*

| | | |
|---|---|---|
| White grape juice | 35fl oz | 1 litre |
| Bananas | 24oz | 680g |
| Peaches | 24oz | 680g |
| Dried apricots | 4oz | 113g |
| Dried figs | 4oz | 113g |
| Dried rosehip shells | 3oz | 85g |
| Raisins | 12oz | 340g |
| Currants | 12oz | 340g |
| Dark muscovado sugar | 4oz | 113g |
| Soft brown sugar | as much as possible | |
| Nutrients | | |
| Pectolase | | |
| Yeast: Gervin no. 3 | | |

Build up the yeast with the white grape juice. Pasteurise the dried fruit in 4 pints of water by heating to above 80°C for 10 minutes, and cooling immediately. Liquidise all the fruit, treat with pectolase, add the muscovado sugar, and ferment on the pulp for 4 days. Strain into a gallon jar, and keep the specific gravity above 1.010 by adding the brown sugar 8oz at a time until the fermentation approaches completion. When racked and clarified, sweeten this high alcohol wine to a specific gravity of about 1.030, adjusting the acidity as required.

## After-dinner Wine, White to Brown
*by John Holgate, Harrow Guild of Winemakers*

| | | |
|---|---|---|
| Apple juice | 35fl oz | 1 litre |
| Sultanas | 32oz | 907g |
| Dried figs | 4oz | 113g |
| Dried apricots | 4oz | 113g |
| Tinned prunes | 16oz | 454g |
| Peeled bananas | 16oz | 454g |
| Oak granules | 0.2oz | 5g |
| Sugar | as much as possible | |
| Pectolase | | |
| Nutrients | | |
| Yeast: Gervin no. 3 | | |

Build up the yeast starter with the apple juice. Wash the dried fruit, stone the prunes, and liquidise all the fruit. Put into a fermentation bin with 16oz dissolved sugar, pectolase, and 5ml 10% metabisulphite. Leave for 24 hours, then add the yeast and nutrients. Ferment on the pulp for 4 days, strain into a gallon jar, and add the oak granules. When the specific gravity drops to 1.010, add 8oz sugar, repeating this addition every time the specific gravity drops to 1.010. When fermentation ceases, add sufficient sugar to make the final specific gravity about 1.030. Rack and clarify using standard techniques. The final wine should attain over 18% alcohol, and have high acidity for the necessary balance.

## After-dinner Wine, White to Brown
*by Bill Smith*

| | | |
|---|---|---|
| White grape juice | 105fl oz | 3 litres |
| Raisins | 8oz | 227g |
| Dates | 8oz | 227g |
| Dried apricots | 4oz | 113g |
| Guava | 6oz | 170g |
| Mango | 4oz | 113g |
| Peach | 8oz | 227g |
| Strawberry | 4oz | 113g |
| Lychee flesh | 2oz | 57g |
| Honey | 4oz | 113g |
| Oak shavings | 1oz | 28g |
| Soft brown sugar | 16oz | 454g |
| White sugar | as much as possible | |
| Pectolase | | |
| Nutrients | | |
| Yeast: Gervin varietal E, strain K1 | | |

The wine is not typical of the amateur winemaker's white after-dinner style, being more like a muscatel style than a Madeira or sherry.

Build up the yeast starter with the white grape juice and the sugar. When most of the sugar has been used up, pasteurise and homogenise the dried fruit, treat with pectolase for 4 hours, and pulp ferment for 2 days. Mash the fresh fruit, and treat with metabisulphite. Add the pasteurised honey to the fresh fruit, and treat with pectolase for 4 hours. Add to the pulp fermentation along with the pasteurised oak shavings, adding more sugar as necessary. Ferment on the pulp for 2 more days, then rack into a gallon jar, and continue the fermentation as long as possible, feeding with sugar to keep the specific gravity above 1.020. Rack and clarify using standard techniques. Depending on the acidity level, the wine can be sweetened to taste with either sugar or white grape concentrate. The wine usually has the best balance when the specific gravity is between 1.030 and 1.040.

### After-dinner Red Wine

Few examples of unfortified after-dinner red wines exist in the commercial world. The common fortified red styles are port and the tawney coloured malmsey. Port is little more than grapes marinated in distilled spirits, while malmsey has been cooked at upwards of 37°C for 3-6 months. The acidity of port tends to be low, while that of malmsey is high.

However, without resorting to fortification, and without the incubators to cook at constant temperatures, the amateur winemaker makes marvellous after-dinner red wines. There are plenty of ingredients that can be used, with grape concentrate and indigenous red fruits being the prime candidates. Pulp fermentations and the appropriate use of oak all contribute to making this high-quality wine. With a high-alcohol yeast and nutrients, about 20% alcohol can be produced.

### After-dinner Red Wine: Mavrodaphne of Patras Style
by Alan Kimber, Harrow Guild of Winemakers

| | | |
|---|---|---|
| Blackberries | 48oz | 1361g |
| Elderberries | 16oz | 454g |
| Raisins | 16oz | 454g |
| Bananas | 8oz | 227g |
| Sugar | 25oz | 709g |
| Tartaric acid | 0.2oz | 5g |
| Bentonite | 0.2oz | 5g |
| Nutrients | | |
| Pectolase | | |
| Yeast: Gervin varietal C | | |

This recipe is designed to give a wine of 16% alcohol, and an acidity between 0.6% and 0.7%.
Mavrodaphne is one of the few examples of an after-dinner commercial wine that is not fortified. Although the commercial is most often found as a red style, it can vary tremendously in colour, and sometimes would be more suited to a white to brown style on the show bench. However, it remains excellent value for money, about £4.00 at the time of writing. Preferably using pre-frozen elderberries, defrost them overnight within a fine straining bag and then press out, since only the expressed juice will be used. The next day, in a suitable fermenting bucket, crush the blackberries with a potato masher, add the minced raisins, the liquidised banana flesh, the elderberries, and the sugar dissolved as sugar syrup. Make the volume up to about 7 pints with boiled water and, when cool, add the nutrient, pectolase, and activated yeast. Two days after fermentation starts, add the bentonite (hydrated if the powdered variety is used). Allow the fermentation to proceed for a further 4 days. Then strain off the must, make up to 1 gallon with water, and

continue the fermentation under an airlock. After fermentation has finished, rack in the normal way, treat with 10ml of 10% metabisulphite solution, and fine as necessary. The finished, clear wine should be sweetened with sugar to a specific gravity of about 1.035.

## After-dinner Red Wine

*by Brenda Holgate, Harrow Guild of Winemakers*

| | | |
|---|---|---|
| Red grape concentrate | 8fl oz | 227ml |
| Sloes | 8oz | 227g |
| Blackberries | 36oz | 1020g |
| Black plums | 16oz | 454g |
| Raspberries | 4oz | 113g |
| Bananas | 16oz | 454g |
| Elderberries | 36oz | 1020g |
| Gervin oak granules | 0.5oz | 14g |
| Nutrients | | |
| Pectolase | | |
| Yeast: Gervin no. 3 | | |

Build up the yeast starter with the diluted red grape concentrate. Mash all the fruit and cover with boiling water in a fermentation bin, although the elderberries benefit from steam extraction in order to soften the tannins. Stir in 8oz sugar, and when cool, treat with pectolase for 4 hours. Add the yeast starter and ferment on the pulp for 4 days. Strain off, add 1.5lbs dissolved sugar, and make the must up to 7 pints with water. When the specific gravity has dropped to 1.000, add a further 1lb sugar and 0.5oz oak granules.

Keep feeding with sugar every time the specific gravity falls to 1.000. When fermentation is complete, rack and clarify using standard procedures. Sweeten to taste with sugar, usually above 1.040. The final wine should have over 18% alcohol, with an acidity between 0.6% and 0.7%.

## After-dinner Red Wine: Port Style

*from 'Wine Recipes for the Connoisseur' by Ted Adcock*

| | | |
|---|---|---|
| Elderberries | 48oz | 1350g |
| Blackberries | 32g | 900g |
| Damsons | 16oz | 450g |
| Raspberries | 4oz | 112g |
| Sugar | 40oz | 1140g |
| Nutrients | | |
| Pectolase | | |
| Yeast: Gervin no. 6, strain 8906 | | |

This recipe is exactly as published, but it benefits tremendously from the addition of 1oz Gervin oak granules during the pulp fermentation. Further oak maturation is also beneficial. Late addition of the blackberries and raspberries enhances the wine's bouquet. As the acidity can finish on the high side, reduction with calcium carbonate or potassium hydrogen carbonate may be required. Red grape concentrate is the recommended sweetener, with the final specific gravity depending on the balance of the wine and the required style. i.e., an after-dinner non-fortified style will probably suit a specific gravity of 1.040-1.050, whereas a fortified port style may be as low as 1.020-1.030.

**After-dinner Red Wine**
by *Chilterns Masters*

| | | |
|---|---|---|
| Red grape concentrate | 20fl oz | 568ml |
| Apple juice | 35fl oz | 1 litre |
| Ribena | 5fl oz | 142ml |
| Elderberries | 24oz | 680g |
| Blackberries | 24oz | 680g |
| Raspberries | 8oz | 227g |
| Honey | 8oz | 227g |
| Mixed white fruit | 32oz | 907g |
| Sugar | as much as possible | |
| Pectolase | | |
| Nutrients | | |
| Yeast: Gervin varietal E, strain K1 | | |

Build up the yeast starter in the red grape concentrate and Ribena in a volume of 4 pints in a gallon jar. Slowly feed in about 16oz sugar. After about a week, pasteurise the red fruit and the honey, treat with pectolase, and pulp ferment adding more sugar as necessary. About 4 days later, mash the white fruit, treat with pectolase and metabisulphite, and add to the pulp fermentation. Next day, strain into a gallon jar, rinse the fruit with water to top up the gallon jar, and ferment to dryness. Rack and clarify using standard procedures. The white fruit is used to improve the fruitiness of the wine without raising tannin levels too high. Although oak was not used in this wine at the time of the recipe formulation, the use of pasteurised oak shavings during the pulp fermentation is recommended. Further oak maturation is also beneficial to this wine. The acidity of this wine can be very high, but it is well balanced by its richness and sweetness, usually being at its best above specific gravity 1.040.

**After-dinner Red Wine**
by *Bill Smith*

| | | |
|---|---|---|
| Red grape concentrate | 15fl oz | 426ml |
| Elderberries | 24oz | 680g |
| Blackberries | 24oz | 680g |
| Blackcurrants | 16oz | 454g |
| Sultanas | 16oz | 454g |
| Peaches | 16oz | 454g |
| Raspberries | 4oz | 113g |
| Strawberries | 4oz | 113g |
| Lychee flesh | 4oz | 113g |
| Oak shavings or granules | 1oz | 28g |
| Sugar | as much as possible | |
| Pectolase | | |
| Nutrients | | |
| Yeast: Gervin varietal E, strain K1 | | |

Build up the yeast starter in diluted grape concentrate. Pasteurise the elderberries, blackberries, blackcurrants, and sultanas, treating with pectolase for 4 hours when cool. Pulp ferment at a volume of 6 pints, adding 16oz of sugar. When most of the sugar has been used, mash the rest of the fruit, treating with pectolase and metabisulphite at 100ppm. Add to the pulp fermentation and continue for 24 hours. Rack into a gallon jar, and continue fermenting, adding sugar to keep the specific gravity above 1.020. Rack and fine using standard techniques. The wine will benefit from further maturation with oak strips for at least 6 months. The wine needs to be sweetened to a specific gravity of at least 1.040 for drinking, and should have over 18% alcohol.

### After-dinner Red Wine
*by Sandra Claydon, Downley Wine Circle*

| | | |
|---|---|---|
| Solvino red grape concentrate | 20fl oz | 568ml |
| Apple juice | 35fl oz | 1 litre |
| Elderberries | 24oz | 680g |
| Blackberries | 16oz | 454g |
| Bottled bilberries | 8oz | 227g |
| Raspberries | 8oz | 227g |
| Blackcurrants | 8oz | 227g |
| Bananas | 8oz | 227g |
| Peach | 8oz | 227g |
| Clear honey | 8oz | 227g |
| Oak shavings | 1oz | 28g |
| Sugar | as much as possible | |
| Nutrients | | |
| Pectolase | | |
| Yeast: Gervin no. 3 | | |

Build up the yeast starter with the apple juice and the red grape concentrate in a volume of 4 pints. Feed with sugar until fermentation slows down. Pasteurise the red fruit, honey, and oak, and mash the red fruit along with the banana and peach. Treat with pectolase, and ferment on the pulp for 4 days. Strain into a gallon jar, and continue the fermentation with sugar additions to keep the specific gravity above 1.010. When fermentation ceases, rack and clarify, sweetening to taste, usually above specific gravity 1.040. Although all the red fruit in this recipe has been added at the same time, the character of the wine can be changed by holding back some of the fruit until very late in the fermentation, as has been discussed in an earlier chapter. This virtual marination of some of the fruit preserves fruitiness, as shown by improved bouquets and flavours.

## Sparkling Wines

Commercially, champagne is the star sparkling wine. However, it is not cheap. Made mainly from Chardonnay and Pinot Noir grapes grown in high latitudes, the wines are high in acidity which may range from 0.6%-0.9%. Secondary fermentation in the bottle produces about 6 atmospheres of pressure in the best commercial wines. As described in the chapter 'Sparkling Wines', the amateur wines described here are designed to produce no more than 4 atmospheres.

To make sparkling wines, the ingredients need to be fresh and fruity. Pulp fermentations are to be avoided, and the primary fermentation should be carried out below 20°C. The secondary fermentation in the bottle should be carried out as described in the chapter 'Sparkling Wines'.

### Sparkling Wine
*by Bill Smith*

| | | |
|---|---|---|
| Vine prunings, frozen fresh shoots | 16oz | 454g |
| Rhubarb, chopped & frozen | 8oz | 227g |
| Gooseberries | 16oz | 454g |
| Strawberries | 2oz | 57g |
| Lychee flesh | 1oz | 28g |
| White grape juice | 35fl oz | 1 litre |
| Apple juice | 18fl oz | 500ml |
| Sugar | 24oz | 680g |
| Nutrients | | |
| Pectolase | | |
| Yeast: Gervin 6, strain 8906 | | |

Build up the yeast starter with the white grape juice, the apple juice, and some of the sugar. The vine prunings should be frozen in a plastic bag immediately after being trimmed. About 2 days after starting the yeast, crush the frozen prunings by stamping on the bag a few times. Extract the prunings by covering them with cold sulphited water and leave overnight, stirring occasionally. Thaw the chopped, frozen rhubarb by covering with sulphited water. Strain the vine prunings and the rhubarb into a gallon jar, add the yeast starter and the rest of the sugar, and ferment at a volume of about 6 pints until most of the sugar has been used. At this stage mash the gooseberries, lychees, and strawberries in 1 pint of water plus pectolase and allow to soak for 2 hours, stirring frequently to allow some, but not extended, skin contact. Strain into the gallon jar, sparge the fruit with water to top up the jar, and ferment to dryness. When racked and clarified, the fermentation in the bottle can be carried out as described in the chapter 'Sparkling

Wines'. When sweetening for the bottle fermentation, this wine is best sweetened with white grape juice, as the alcohol is already about 12%, and this treatment will keep the sparkling wine at this alcohol level. Remember that, at the disgorging stage, it pays to have kept back some of the base wine to top up the wine before resealing the bottle. This avoids the possibility of precipitation due to incompatibilities if using two different wines.

### Sparkling Wine
*by Bill Smith*

| | | |
|---|---|---|
| Rhubarb, chopped & frozen | 32oz | 907g |
| Apple juice | 35fl oz | 1 litre |
| Elderflower and grape concentrate | 5fl oz | 142ml |
| Peaches | 4oz | 113g |
| Guavas | 2oz | 57g |
| Mangos | 2oz | 57g |
| Sugar | 18oz | 510g |
| Nutrients | | |
| Pectolase | | |
| Yeast: Gervin 6, strain 8906 | | |

Start the yeast in the apple juice, then build it up over a few days with the diluted elderflower and grape concentrate. Thaw the chunks of frozen rhubarb in cold sulphited water, strain the juice through a sieve with a light pressing, treat with pectolase, and add to the yeast starter along with the sugar. Ferment this in·a gallon jar at a volume of about 6 pints until most of the sugar has been used. Mash the fruit in a pint of water, add pectolase, soak with stirring for 2 hours, then strain into the gallon jar, rinsing the fruit with water to top up the jar. Ferment to dryness, and, when clear, proceed with the bottle fermentation as described in the chapter 'Sparkling Wines'. As the alcohol in the base wine here is less than 11%, the wine can be sweetened for the bottle fermentation with sugar, although subtle variations can be obtained by sweetening with grape concentrate or white grape juice. Some of the original still wine should be held back for the dosage.

### Sparkling Wine: Blanc de Blanc Style
*by Bill Smith*

| | | |
|---|---|---|
| White grape concentrate | 16fl oz | 455ml |
| Apple juice | 35fl oz | 1 litre |
| Bananas | 4oz | 113g |
| Mangos | 12oz | 340g |
| Peaches | 4oz | 113g |
| Strawberries | 2oz | 57g |
| Sugar | 16oz | 454g |
| Nutrients | | |
| Pectolase | | |
| Yeast: Gervin 6, strain 8906 | | |

This wine has Chardonnay style, and is always well appreciated on the show bench. The concentrate should be grape only, and should not be caramelised. Build up the yeast with the apple juice, white grape concentrate, and sugar in a total volume of 6 pints. When most of the sugar has been used, mash the fruit, treat with pectolase and metabisulphite at 100ppm, and pulp ferment for 2 hours. Strain into a gallon jar, rinsing the fruit with water. Top up with water, and ferment to dryness. Rack and clarify by standard techniques, and proceed as in the chapter 'Sparkling Wines'. The wine is best sweetened with white grape juice for the bottle fermentation. Some of the original still wine should be held back for the dosage.

### Sparkling Wine: Medium Sweet Rosé
*by Bill Smith*

| | | |
|---|---|---|
| White grape juice | 70fl oz | 2 litres |
| Apple juice | 35fl oz | 1 litre |
| Nectarines | 8oz | 227g |
| Sugar | 16oz | 454g |
| Sweetened raspberry juice | 1.2fl oz | 34ml |
| Nutrients | | |
| Pectolase | | |
| Yeast: Gervin 6, strain 8906 | | |

Build up the yeast starter with the white grape concentrate, apple juice, and sugar to a volume of 6 pints in a gallon jar. When most of the sugar has been used, mash the nectarines and treat with pectolase. Strain the juice from the mashed nectarines into the gallon jar, rinsing the pulp with water to top up the jar. Ferment to dryness, and proceed with the bottle fermentation when the wine has cleared. After disgorging, top up the bottle with 34ml sweetened raspberry juice, plus more wine if required. To make the raspberry juice, extract and clarify the juice from fresh or frozen raspberries. This can be done using a domestic juice extractor, or by simply mashing and straining the fruit. The fruit may need pectolase treatment for starbright clarity. Add sugar and dissolve until the juice is saturated. It is useful to make a large batch which can be frozen in 34ml aliquots. It is essential to have this juice about freezing point before starting the disgorging process, as this will keep any frothing to a minimum when the dosage is added. This wine is a delight at any time, but excels on a summer afternoon.

### Sparkling Wine: Elderflower Style
*by Bill Smith*

| | | |
|---|---|---|
| Apple juice | 35fl oz | 1 litre |
| Elderflower and grape concentrate | 26fl oz | 739ml |
| Sugar | 8oz | 227g |
| Pectolase | | |
| Nutrients | | |
| Yeast: Gervin 6, strain 8906 | | |

This is an easily-made wine, which has surprisingly good quality. Build up the yeast in the apple juice, treating with pectolase. When fermentation is proceeding well, transfer to a gallon jar along with the diluted concentrate and the dissolved sugar. When fermented to dryness, rack and clarify by standard techniques, and proceed as in the chapter 'Sparkling Wines'. The wine is best sweetened with white grape juice for the bottle fermentation. Some of the original still wine should be held back for the dosage.

### Country Wines

These are wines that stem from the early days of home winemaking. The recipes below all make very interesting wines, which sometimes are not suitable for any class on the show bench. Maybe this should be rectified, with more being done to preserve these interesting old styles.

### Country Wine: Apple and Elderflower

*from 'Home Winemaking the Right Way' by Ken Hawkins, published by Elliot Right Way Books*

| | | |
|---|---|---|
| White grape concentrate | 10fl oz | 284ml |
| Apple juice | 35fl oz | 1 litre |
| Fresh elderflower florets | 10fl oz | (1 cup), 284ml |
| Sugar | 28oz | 794g |
| Citric acid | 0.35oz | 10g |
| Nutrients | | |
| Pectolase | | |
| Yeast: Gervin no. 6, strain 8906 | | |

The same ingredients have been used as in Home Winemaking The Right Way, but the order in which they are added has been amended in order to enhance the elderflower aroma. Build up the yeast starter with diluted white grape concentrate. After 2 days, add the rest of the ingredients except the elderflower, and ferment in a gallon jar about 80% full. When most of the sugar has been used, sterilise the elderflowers in 15fl oz water sulphited with 2ml 10% metabisulphite for 2 hours. Transfer the elderflowers into a fermenting bin, and add the liquid in the gallon jar. Strain back into the gallon jar after 1 day, top up with water, and ferment to dryness. As the alcohol of the base wine is quite high at about 14%, the wine is best sweetened just before use with white grape juice, the wine drinking as a medium wine with 12-13% alcohol and about 0.5% acidity. In making a wine like this, where it is best to add fresh elderflower, the wine should be started at least a week before the elderflowers are picked and added. Thus all the attractive fragrance of elderflower is found in the bouquet of the wine.

**Country Wine: Orange Wine**
by Sandra Claydon, Downley Wine Circle

| | | |
|---|---|---|
| Oranges | 10 | 10 |
| Orange juice | 35fl oz | 1 litre |
| Bananas | 12oz | 340g |
| Sultanas | 32oz | 907g |
| Light brown sugar | 32oz | 907g |
| Nutrients | | |
| Pectolase | | |
| Yeast: Gervin no. 6, strain 8906 | | |

Build up the yeast starter with the orange juice. Peel the oranges, crush the flesh, liquidise the sultanas and banana, and treat with metabisulphite and pectolase. Pulp ferment for 2 days at a volume of about 5 pints, adding the boiled peel from 5 of the oranges. Strain into a gallon jar, and feed with sugar until fermentation ceases. When racked and clarified, this will be a high alcohol, low acidity wine. Sweeten to taste with white grape juice or white grape concentrate, the wine being at its best between specific gravity 1.030 and 1.040.

**Country Wine: Spiced Banana**
by Bob Hawtin, Booker Wine Circle

| | | |
|---|---|---|
| Peeled banana | 4lbs | 1814g |
| Dried rosehip shells | 4oz | 113g |
| White grape concentrate | 10fl oz | 284ml |
| Demerara sugar | 2.5lbs | 1134g |
| Ground cloves | 0.2oz | 6g |
| Mixed spices | 0.2oz | 6g |
| Chopped ginger | 0.2oz | 6g |
| Tartaric acid | 0.4oz | 11g |
| Nutrients | | |
| Pectolase | | |
| Yeast: Gervin no. 3 | | |

This is a high-alcohol, low-acidity wine, in which the spices help to maintain the balance of the wine. Build the yeast up with the diluted white grape concentrate to a volume of 2 pints. Boil the bananas in 4 pints water for 30 minutes, then strain over the rosehips and sugar, leaving to cool for 2 hours. Strain into a gallon jar and add the pectolase, cloves, spices, and ginger. When racked and clarified, add sugar to the required level of taste, usually between specific gravity 1.010 and 1.020.

**Country Wine: Blackberry and Apple**
from 'Home Winemaking the Right Way' by Ken Hawkins, published by Elliot Right Way Books

| | | |
|---|---|---|
| Blackberries | 48oz | 1361g |
| Apples, mixed | 64oz | 1814g |
| Sugar | 40oz | 1134g |
| Citric acid | 0.2oz | 6g |
| Pectolase | | |
| Nutrients | | |
| Yeast: Gervin no. 6, strain 8906 | | |

Start the yeast in 4fl oz white grape juice. Dissolve the sugar in 2 pints of hot water. Chop the washed apples into a fermentation bin containing the dissolved sugar and 5ml 10% metabisulphite. Mash the blackberries, add them to the apples and sugar, and leave for 24 hours. Add the acid, nutrients, pectolase, and yeast starter, and ferment on the pulp for 5 days at a volume of 7 pints, stirring frequently. Strain into a gallon jar, top up with water, and ferment to dryness. Rack and clarify using standard techniques. The wine should be ready for drinking within 4 months, and should be sweetened to taste, usually about specific gravity 1.010. This will give a high alcohol wine with 0.7-0.9% acidity.

## Country wine: Fruit Red Sweet
### by Bill Smith

| | | |
|---|---|---|
| White grape juice | 35fl oz | 1 litre |
| Blackberries | 96oz | 2721g |
| Raspberries | 8oz | 227g |
| Peaches | 32oz | 907g |
| Sugar | 32oz | 907g |
| Pectolase | | |
| Nutrients | | |
| Yeast: Gervin 6, strain 8906 | | |

Start the yeast with the white grape juice. After 2 days, pasteurise the blackberries and the raspberries, blanch the peaches and remove their skins and stones. Mash all the fruit, and treat with pectolase for 4 hours. Dissolve the sugar, and ferment on the pulp at a volume of 7 pints for 4 days. Strain into a gallon jar, and rinse the fruit with 1 pint water. Top up with water, and ferment to dryness, or until fermentation ceases. Rack and clarify as usual. If all the sugar is fermented the wine will be about 16% alcohol. Sweeten to taste with sugar, grape concentrate, or grape juice. This is a very fruity wine, worth a show entry as a sweet fruit wine. Holding back some of the fruit until the fermentation is nearing completion can enhance the fruitiness of the wine.